The Keys to the CATW

Third Edition

Regina A. Rochford
Associate Professor
Queensborough Community College, CUNY

publishing company

Cover image © Shutterstock, Inc.

Kendall Hunt
publishing company

www.kendallhunt.com
Send all inquiries to:
4050 Westmark Drive
Dubuque, IA 52004-1840

In memory of my parents

Agnes R. Rochford and

Martin X. Rochford

Gone, but never forgotten

Thanks for making me what I am!

Table of Contents

Aim of the CATW 1

Purpose of the Guidebook 1

Chapter One 2

    Drafting a Summary 2

    Overview 2

    The Reading Passage... 3

    Determining the Main Idea 4

    Summary Writing 5

    Practice Summarizing 10

    Error Analysis 19

    Answer Key for Chapter One 29

Chapter Two 30

    Organizing Your Essay 30

    Determining Key Ideas for Discussion 30

        Selecting One Key Idea for Discussion 30

        Practice Turning Key Ideas into Thesis Statements and Questions . 31

    Drafting the Introduction 32

        Error Analyses of Introduction Paragraphs 33

    Writing Effective Topic Sentences 35

        Composing Topic Sentences 36

        Varying Vocabulary 37

        Practice Creating Topic Sentences 37

    Error Analyses of Topic Sentences 38

    Outlining the Essay 39

    Writing the Essay 40

    Body Paragraph Development 42

        Techniques Used to Develop Body Paragraphs 42

        Transition Words 43

        Practice Using Transition Words 43

Practice Identifying the Type of Supporting Details Used 44

Practice Writing Supporting Details 45

Error Analysis of Supporting Details 46

The Conclusion Paragraph 52

The Entire Essay 53

Error Analysis of Conclusion Paragraph 55

Your Turn to Practice Writing a CATW Essay 57

Selecting One Key Idea for Discussion 57

Creating a Thesis Question 57

Stating your Thesis and Writing a Summary 58

Using the Thesis Question to Brainstorm Ideas for the Body

Paragraphs 58

Writing Topic Sentences 59

Writing Your Essay 59

Answer Key for Chapter Two 60

Chapter Three 63

Passage One: 63

Disruptions: Life's Too Short for So Much E-Mail 63

Passage Two 64

Cell Phones and Driving 64

Passage Three 65

Study: Facebook Users Are Friendlier 65

Passage Four 65

Advantages of Community Colleges 65

Passage Five 66

An E-Book Fan, Missing the Smell of Paper and Glue 66

Passage Six 68

College Students Behaving Badly 68

Passage Seven 69

Texting While Walking 69

Passage Eight 69

Is College for Everyone? 69

Passage Nine   70

No Junk Food in Schools! 70

Passage Ten   71

Spoiled Children 71

Passage Eleven   72

College Athletes and Academics 72

Passage Twelve   73

Spoiled Brats 73

Passage Thirteen   73

What You've Never Had, You Never Miss: Canadian Couple who

Won $11.2m in the Lottery Gives It ALL away to Charity 73

Passage Fourteen   74

Why Must I Take these Courses? 74

Passage Fifteen   75

Hearing Loss among Young People 75

Passage Sixteen   76

Is Multitasking Productive? 76

Passage Seventeen   77

Moving Often Impacts Children 77

Passage Eighteen   78

How to Study Effectively 78

Passage Nineteen   79

Going on a Diet? Start Paying in Cash 79

Passage Twenty   80

Achieving a Healthful Digital Diet 80

Chapter Four ....

Language Use on the CATW 82

Independent Clauses 82

Conjunctive Adverbs and the Semi-Colon 84

Using Conjunctive Adverbs to Convey the Correct Meaning 85

Error Analysis 86

Dependent Adverbial Clauses 87

    Practice Exercise 88

Verb Tenses 90

    Present Tense 90

        Non-count Nouns and the Present Tense 91

        Gerunds and the Present Tense 91

        Indefinite Pronouns and the Present Tense 92

        Practice Exercise 92

        Practice in Context 93

    The Present Progressive Tense 93

        Practice Exercise 94

    The Past Tense 95

        Irregular Verbs in the Past Tense 96

        Frequent Errors in the Use of Irregular Past Tense Verbs 96

        Error Analysis 98

  Vocabulary 99

  Answer Key for Chapter Four 102

Appendix A: Irregular Verbs 104

References 108

Aim of the CATW

The purpose of the CUNY Assessment Test in Writing (CATW) is to determine if you can read, understand, evaluate, critique, and write at the college level.

Purpose of the Guidebook

The goal of this guidebook is to assist you in writing an effective, passing CATW exam. Therefore, it will direct you through the process of:

- reading a passage,

- determining the key ideas,

- writing and paraphrasing a summary,

- selecting one key idea for discussion in your essay,

- drafting an outline,

- writing a critical response in the form of an essay, and

- editing your essay.

Answer Keys

As you progress through this guidebook, you will be asked many questions so that you can develop an understanding of what is expected on this test and avoid typical mistakes that developmental writers make. Therefore, to help you verify your knowledge, the answers to each question are numbered and provided at the end of each chapter.

Additional Readings

The first chapter of this book provides six reading passages that permit you to practice reading, summarizing and writing. In order to afford you sufficient practice, Chapter Three contains additional reading passages that can be used to practice the skills you learned in this book.

Chapter One

Drafting a Summary

Overview

The first part of the CATW exam requires you to determine the key ideas of a reading passage and write a summary.

1. The CATW test will provide a short reading and then ask you to respond by using the following instructions.

   Read the passage and write an essay responding to the ideas it presents. In your essay, be sure to summarize the passage in your own words, stating the author's most important ideas. Develop your essay by identifying one idea in the passage that you feel is especially significant, and explain its significance. Support your claims with evidence or examples drawn from what you have read, learned in school, and/or personally experienced. Remember to review your essay and make any changes or corrections that will help your reader follow your thinking. You will have 90 minutes to complete your essay.

2. What do these instructions tell you to do? These instructions expect you to:

   a. read a passage;

   b. create a summary that contains the key ideas in a passage.

   c. identify one key idea that you will discuss.

   d. explain the significance or importance of the key idea you've selected and provide supporting details to develop your ideas.

   e. review and edit your essay so that it is grammatical, clear and easy to understand.

   f. all of the above [1]

3. In most reading classes, your instructors will explain that the key idea or the most important idea in a reading passage is called:

   a. the main idea

b. the supporting details

c. inferences

d. facts and statistics [2]

4. In addition to the main idea in a reading class, the other important points that an author makes are referred to as:

a. the supporting details

b. facts

c. the major details

d. all of the above. [3]

5. Therefore, when you draft your summary, you must include the key ideas. For the purpose of the CATW exam, the key ideas of a passage include:

a. examples

b. statistics

c. quotes and definitions

d. main idea and the major details [4]

The Reading Passage

The following sample reading passage will be used to demonstrate how to write a passing CATW essay in this book.

Read the following practice reading passage. Then follow the instructions below.

Distracted: Are you paying $75 an hour to sit in class and check Facebook? [i]

Look around any college classroom these days and you'll see students who are focused and attentive – though not necessarily on the curriculum. A study by psychology professors at Wilkes University found that 91 percent of students admit to having used their phones to text during class, even though one third of those surveyed agreed that the student sending the message would be affected "through a loss of attention and/or poor grades in the class."

This rise in technological distractions has frustrated many university professors, including Santa Clara English professor Heather Julien, who has been teaching First Year Writing for almost 15 years. Julien says that she has always supported the use of technology in the classroom, but that the increase in the number of students texting and using Facebook has brought her close to banning electronics from her classes.

Not all professors find that technology is to blame for students' short attention spans. A recent study from chemistry professors at The Catholic University of America in Washington, DC revealed that a student's difficulty in maintaining focus may be due to human nature. While previous studies found that students were able to maintain focus for periods of 10-20 minutes during lectures, the Catholic study discovered that students actually "alternate between being engaged and non-engaged in ever-shortening cycles throughout a lecture segment." The study found that students reported attention lapsed as early as 30 seconds into a lecture and could bounce back and forth between engagement and non-engagement in intervals as short as two or three minutes.

Dr. Diane Bunce is a chemistry educator at Catholic University who studies why people struggle learning the discipline and one of the professors who conducted the attention study. According to Bunce, the ability of students to focus and learn in the classroom depends not only on their own personal motivation, but also on the teaching methods employed by the professor.

But regardless of a distraction's cause, students who spend precious classroom minutes out of focus are also failing to maximize the thousands of dollars spent on university tuition fees. And with a college degree a necessity in today's competitive workforce, students are perhaps taking their classroom experience for granted, said Julien. "In this day and age of virtually required higher education," she said, "a lot of those folks may not have a great intrinsic value of education."

Determining the Main Idea

1. The **topic** of a reading passage is usually a few words that express the general subject being discussed.

    What is the topic of this passage?

    a. the increase in the cost of a college education

    b. the increase in text messaging and social networking in college classes

4

c. the decreased use of technology among college professors

d. the decline in focus of students in college classes [5]

2.   Next, the **main idea** of a passage summarizes the entire reading, and it usually contains the topic and the author's opinion or the point being made. It is also expressed in as one complete sentence.

What is the main idea of this passage?

a. American colleges are becoming too costly for students.

b. College students have become adept at texting and using social networks while they are in class.

c. Many college instructors are concerned by students who text and check social networks while they are in class.

d. Students can't focus in college classes because their professors employ boring teaching techniques.

e. College students are unable to pay attention in class because their attention spans are too short. [6]

Summary Writing

The CATW exam requests you compose a summary that contains the key ideas, which means you must include the main idea and the major details. However, it doesn't demand that you include every single major detail. Therefore, you should simply focus on determining the main idea and a couple of the major details. Observe the process used to summarize the following passage.

1.   After you read the passage a couple of times, highlight the main idea and major details in this passage. This means you do NOT include supporting details such as statistics, examples, stories, quotes, definitions.

Distracted: Are you paying $75 an hour sit in class and check Facebook?

Look around any college classroom these days and you'll see students who are focused and attentive – though not necessarily on the curriculum. A study by psychology professors at Wilkes

University found that 91 percent of students admit to having used their phones to text during class, even though one third of those surveyed agreed that the student sending the message would be affected "through a loss of attention and/or poor grades in the class."

This rise in technological distractions has frustrated many university professors, including Santa Clara English professor Heather Julien, who has been teaching First Year Writing for almost 15 years. Julien says that she has always supported the use of technology in the classroom, but that the increase in the number of students texting and using Facebook has brought her close to banning electronics from her classes.

Not all professors find that technology is to blame for students' short attention spans. A recent study from chemistry professors at The Catholic University of America in Washington, DC revealed that a student's difficulty in maintaining focus may be due to human nature. While previous studies found that students were able to maintain focus for periods of 10-20 minutes during lectures, the Catholic study discovered that students actually "alternate between being engaged and non-engaged in ever-shortening cycles throughout a lecture segment." The study found that students reported attention lapsed as early as 30 seconds into a lecture and could bounce back and forth between engagement and non-engagement in intervals as short as two or three minutes.

Dr. Diane Bunce is a chemistry educator at Catholic University who studies why people struggle learning the discipline and one of the professors who conducted the attention study. According to Bunce, the ability of students to focus and learn in the classroom depends not only on their own personal motivation, but also on the teaching methods employed by the professor.

But regardless of a distraction's cause, students who spend precious classroom minutes out of focus are also failing to maximize the thousands of dollars spent on university tuition fees. And with a college degree a necessity in today's competitive workforce, students are perhaps taking their classroom experience for granted, said Julien. "In this day and age of virtually required higher education," she said, "a lot of those folks may not have a great intrinsic value of education."

2. Use the highlighted sentences to draft a summary. However, as you copy the highlighted sections, you must make certain to write in complete sentences so that your summary makes sense. Observe how this step is completed below.

~~This rise in~~ *T*echnological distractions ha*ve* frustrated many university professors, *because of t*he increase in the number of students' texting and using Facebook *during class*. Students' difficulty in maintaining focus may be due to human nature. *Th*e ability of students to focus and learn in the classroom depends not only on their own personal motivation, but also on the teaching

6

methods employed by the professor. *Students who spend precious classroom minutes out of focus are also failing to maximize the thousands of dollars spent on university tuition fees.*

3.   What is paraphrasing?

Paraphrasing refers to:

a.   copying another person's exact words to express an idea.

b.   using different words and language to express what was stated in the passage.

c.   plagiarizing or using another person's words illegally.

d.   none of the above [7]

4.   Observe how this summary is paraphrased.

~~Technological distractions have frustrated~~ *Many* ~~university professors~~ *college instructors are discouraged,* because of the ~~increase~~ *rise* in the number of students *who send* text~~ing~~ *messages* and ~~using~~ *check* ~~Facebook~~ *social networks* during class. ~~Students' difficulty in maintaining focus may be due to human nature.~~ *Many learners have trouble paying attention in class since* ~~losing focus is due to human nature~~ *it is human nature to lose focus.* The ability of students to ~~focus~~ *concentrate* and learn in the classroom ~~depends~~ *varies according to* ~~not only on~~ their own ~~personal~~ *individual* motivation~~, but~~ *and* also on the ~~teaching methods employed~~ *pedagogy used* by the professor. Students who ~~spend precious classroom minutes out of focus~~ *don't pay attention during class* ~~are also failing to maximize~~ *waste the money they spend* ~~on the thousands of dollars spent on university~~ *on* tuition ~~fees~~.

Caution for ESL Learners: When you paraphrase, be certain to use the correct part of speech and a word or words with the correct meaning. This can be accomplished by using an English dictionary and/or a thesaurus. When students use translation dictionaries, they frequently select a word that is not the correct part of speech. For instance, they might insert an adjective instead of verb or a word with a completely different meaning. For this reason, it is suggested that you avoid translation devices.

5.   What are transition words?

If you re-read the paraphrased summary, you will notice that it is chopped up because the sentences do not easily connect to each other. To correct this problem, skilled writers insert transitions words, which make their writing smooth and easy to read. However, transition words must express the correct meaning. For this reason, the next section will explain the basic meaning of several commonly used transition words.

Respond to the following questions about transition words.

6.   What are transition words? They are words used to:

    a. prevent plagiarizing the author's original words.

    b. create a smooth connection from one written idea to the next.

    c. add details to a sentence and essay. [8]

7.   Can you select the transition words that refer to providing additional information?

    a. however, on the other hand, in contrast

    b. in addition, furthermore, additionally, moreover, and, also

    c. therefore, thus, as a result, consequently [9]

8.   Can you identify some transition words that refer to a contrast or a difference?

    a. however, on the other hand, in contrast, but, nevertheless, conversely

    b. in addition, furthermore, additionally, moreover, also, besides

    c. therefore, thus, as a result, consequently, so

    d. all of these

    e. b and c [10]

9.   Can you specify transition words that signal that a result or consequence is about to be stated?

a. however, on the other hand; in contrast, but, nevertheless, conversely

b. in addition, furthermore, additionally, moreover, also, besides

c. therefore, thus, as a result, consequently, so

d. all of these [11]

10. Can you indicate some transition words that signal a sequence of events?

    a. first, second

    b. next, then, subsequently

    c. recently, in the years to come

    d. previously

    e. finally

    f. all of these [12]

11. Using Transition Words

Observe how transition words and other minor revisions make this summary clear, concise and connected. These modifications allow you to link one thought to the next, so that your summary is easy to read and understand.

> Many college instructors are discouraged because of the rise in the number of students who send text messages and check social networks during class. *In fact, one study suggests that this occurs because* many learners have trouble paying attention in class since losing focus is part of human nature. *Moreover, t*he ability of students to concentrate and learn in the classroom varies according to their own individual motivation and also on the pedagogy used by the professor. *Finally, the author indicates that when* students ~~who~~ don't pay attention ~~in~~ *during* class*, they* waste the money they spend on tuition.

12. Although you have drafted a summary, it is also necessary to incorporate a reference to the title of the passage and the author if his/her name is provided. Observe how this information has been included in the summary.

> *According to Kurt Wagner in "Distracted: Are you paying $75 an hour sit in class and check Facebook,"* many college instructors are discouraged because of the rise in the number of students who send text messages and check social networks during class. One study suggests that this occurs because many learners have trouble paying attention in class since losing focus is part of human nature. Moreover, the ability of students to concentrate and learn in the classroom varies according to their own individual motivation and also on the pedagogy used by the professor. Finally, the author indicates that when students don't pay attention during class, they waste the money they spend on tuition.

13. In the summary listed above, underline the phrase that the writer added in order to include the title of the passage and a reference to the author. [13]

14. In order to present the title correctly, you should:

   a. capitalize the first letter of each word in the title.

   b. place quotation marks before and after the title.

   c. italicize each word in the title.

   d. a and b [14]

Practice Summarizing

Read each of the following passages and then follow the instructions that follow them.

Practice Passage One

Married Women Who Work Are Happier

Although the trend of working women has required some adjustments, a recent study has demonstrated that when women are employed, their divorce rate decreases. That is when married women work, these couples maintain happier, more stable marriages. However, these results conflict with the traditional belief that financially independent women are more likely to divorce, and that they threaten the stability of a marriage.

The researchers noted that in the 1970s, the divorce rate was 23 in 1,000 couples, whereas it is presently 17 in 1,000. On the other hand, in areas where fewer wives work, the divorce rates are much higher. These statistics suggest that employed women are more likely to stay married.

10

Psychologists believe that the lower divorce rate occurs because independent women shift the balance of power and ease financial issues in the marriage. In addition, these women can be more selective when they choose a husband, and once they are married, they have more input into family decisions, while their husbands benefit from their salaries and fewer money concerns.

One problem these marriages encounter is that the husband and wife must adjust their roles. For instance, some husbands may feel uncomfortable with their wives' authority or with performing household chores. In contrast, many women wrestle with surrendering control of their children and their house. Ironically, although some men expected to be demeaned by their new roles, many indicated that they enjoyed the praise they received from other mothers who admired their flexibility and contributions to their families.

a. State the topic of this passage.

_____

_____

b. State the main idea of this passage in a sentence.

_____

_____

_____

c. Highlight the major details presented in this article. This means you do NOT include supporting details.

d. Use the highlighted sections to draft a summary.

_____

_____

_____

_____

_____

_____

_____

e. Paraphrase your summary.

_____

_____

_____

_____

_____

_____

_____

_____

f. Revise and edit your summary to make it clear and concise. Be certain to include the title of the passage in quotation marks, and a reference to the author. Then, add transition words and make other minor revisions, so that one thought readily connects to the next and your summary is easy to read and understand.

_____

_____

_____

_____

_____

_____

_____

_____

_____

Practice Passage Two

Social Promotion and Retention

In many elementary schools in the United States, even when students cannot earn passing scores, they are promoted to the next grade, despite the fact they are not prepared. This practice is referred to as social promotion, and it is defined as passing students from grade to grade with their peers, even though they are failing. It is called *social* because it is carried out in the interest of a child's social and psychological health. Many researchers, however, contend that promoting unprepared children does not improve their achievement or psychological outlook. At the same time, other studies have also demonstrated that retention, requiring a child to repeat a grade, frequently has negative educational and psychological consequences.

The U.S. Department of Education concluded that social promotion and retention are unsuccessful in improving students' performance. In fact, both policies lead to high dropout rates, especially among low-income, minority students, and they result in an inadequate core of educational skills. Moreover, because retention typically requires a student to repeat a grade with little or no change in the curriculum and teaching methods, it sets the child up for repeated failure. Social promotion has also been criticized because parents, teachers and employers argue that it is worse for a child who is struggling academically to be promoted to the next grade than it is to be left back.

Since social promotion and retention are both viewed as unattractive options, many parents and educators desire the development of more personalized approaches such as: extended school years; alternative schools for special learners; better teacher training programs; early childhood intervention programs; and, prevention programs.

    a. State the topic of this passage.

    _____

    _____

    b. State the main idea of this passage in a sentence.

    _____

    _____

    _____

    c. Highlight the major details presented in this article. This means you do NOT include supporting details.

13

d. Use the highlighted sections to draft a summary that: a) includes the title of the article and the author's name, b) contains the main idea and few major details, c) is paraphrased, d) uses transitions, and e) connects one thought to the next so that your summary is easy to read and understand.

_____

_____

_____

_____

_____

_____

_____

_____

_____

_____

Practice Passage Three

Driving Safety Programs for Teens

Teenagers have more car accidents and driving fatalities than any other age group because they greatly misjudge risky driving situations. However, injury prevention programs can improve their awareness slightly.

Approximately three hundred high-school students participated in a one-day injury prevention program. In addition to discussions about safety, the students toured an intensive care unit at a hospital and met young people who had suffered mild brain or spinal cord injuries in car accidents.

Before they took part in the program, a control group of teens completed a survey about driving safety. The results implied that teenage drivers consistently underestimated driving risks. They believed that most fatal crashes resulted because of car, weather, or highway problems, instead of mistakes in judgment. They also believed that their youthful quickness gave them an edge over experienced drivers in dealing with poor driving conditions.

14

In contrast, the teenagers who participated in the safety program developed more appropriate insights into dangers on the road. However, this knowledge diminished after a few weeks because those who responded to the survey eight days after the safety program obtained higher scores than those who answered it a month later. This study indicates that teen drivers should be reminded frequently that poor judgment and inexperience increase the risk of serious injuries and death.

a. State the topic of this passage.

_____

_____

b. State the main idea of this passage in a sentence.

_____

_____

_____

c. Highlight the main idea and major details presented in this article. This means you do NOT include supporting details.

d. Use the highlighted sections to draft a summary that: a) includes the title of the article and the author's name, b) contains the main idea and a few major details, c) is paraphrased, d) uses transitions, and e) connects one thought to the next so that your summary is easy to read and understand.

_____

_____

_____

_____

_____

_____

_____

_____

_____

_____

Practice Passage Four

Advertisements on Tobacco Products

A new law will require more noticeable health warnings on advertisements for cigarettes and smokeless tobacco products. Until recently, these warnings appeared in tiny print in a small corner of these ads. As a result, many consumers failed to notice them. However, the new ads must fill twenty percent of the advertisement's space so that viewers cannot miss the warnings.

Many advertising experts do not believe that the larger warnings will have a significant impact on consumers. First, even though the warning is bigger, it doesn't necessarily make it more effective or noticeable. Next, the new warnings will appear in white print with a black background, even though consumers tend to focus more on the blue sections of an advertisement because they are more calming.

In addition, since cigarette smoking has declined in this country, the tobacco industry has been accused of using smokeless tobacco to attract new customers, by emphasizing that these products can be used in places that forbid smoking. However, these ads don't mention that smokeless tobacco products can cause cancer of the lips, tongue, cheek, gums, and mouth, not to mention nicotine addiction.

Therefore, in addition to new requirements for cigarette advertisements, packages of cigarettes and smokeless tobacco must increase the size of their warnings and make the language stronger. The warnings on packages containing tobacco must cover the top half of the front and back of each container, and they must provide colorful graphics that describe the health risks associated with tobacco use. In response to these new laws, many tobacco companies have filed lawsuits claiming that these laws interfere with their right to free speech because consumers are already well aware of the dangers that tobacco presents.

a. State the topic of this passage.

_____

_____

b. State the main idea of this passage in a sentence.

_____

_____

c. Highlight the major details presented in this article. This means you do NOT include supporting details.

d. Use the highlighted sections to draft a summary that: a) includes the title of the article and the author's name, b) contains the main idea and few major details, c) is paraphrased, d) uses transitions, and e) connects one thought to the next so that your summary is easy to read and understand.

_____

_____

_____

_____

_____

_____

_____

_____

_____

_____

_____

_____

_____

Practice Passage Five ꓕ·ꓪ

Television Commercials and Obesity among Children

For years, doctors have claimed that too much time in front of the television increases childhood obesity. However, a recent study has demonstrated that it is not the act of looking at a television screen that is the problem, but the commercials that children view.

overweight *explain*

Approximately 2,000 children were observed to determine the amount of time they dedicated to watching television programs. Although the researchers expected to find that children who watched a lot of television would be overweight, they discovered that the chance of being obese increased when

very fat

children watched many television commercials. These results suggest that advertisements for sugary

17

cereals, junk food and fast food influenced children's eating habits because the more television commercials a child looked at, the more likely he or she was to sample these foods and to keep eating them. Thus, these youngsters increased their risk for weight gain.

Over the years, advertisers have developed ingenious [intellegent] ways to attract customers and build food loyalty [cause] by drawing in children when they are young. In fact, this age group is exposed to roughly 30 hours of food promotions annually, and during Saturday cartoons, every five minutes children view advertisements for foods, most of which are fattening. [to make fat]

For many years, it was believed that children who watched a lot of television were prone [tendency to something] to obesity because they lacked physical activity, but this report suggests this theory is not necessarily true. Therefore, there was no evidence of a "couch potato" [a person whose leisure time is spent watching television.] effect.

a. State the topic of this passage.

_____

_____

b. State the main idea of this passage in a sentence.

_____

_____

_____

c. Highlight the major details presented in this article. This means you do NOT include supporting details.

d. Use the highlighted sections to draft a summary that: a) includes the title of the article and the author's name, b) contains the main idea and few major details, c) is paraphrased, d) uses transitions, and e) connects one thought to the next so that your summary is easy to read and understand.

_____

_____

_____

_____

_____

_____

_____

_____

_____

_____

_____

_____

Error Analyses

Read the following summary written about Practice Passage One. Then answer the questions that follow to explain what is incorrect.

> [1] According to the author of "Married Women Who Work Are Happier," when women are employed, the divorce rate among them decreases. [2] However, these results conflict with the traditional belief that financially independent women are more likely to divorce, and that they threaten the stability of a marriage. [3] In the 1970s, the divorce rate was 23 in 1,000 couples, whereas it is presently 17 in 1,000. [4] The lower divorce rate occurs because independent women shift the balance of power and ease financial issues in the marriage. [5] One problem these marriages encounter is that the husband and wife must adjust their roles.

1. The author of this summary:

   a. did not include the main idea.

   b. omitted most of the major details.

   c. included a supporting detail.

   d. changed the meaning of the passage. [15]

2. Use the numbers provided before each sentence in the summary to point out the sentence that should be omitted because it is a supporting detail.

   a. 1

b. 2

c. 3

d. 4

e. 5 [16]

3. What else has been done incorrectly in this summary? The writer:

a. did not paraphrase.

b. copied the exact words in the passage, which is plagiarism.

c. provided inaccurate information in the summary.

d. a and b [17]

Read the following summary written for Practice Passage Two. Then answer the questions that follow to explain what has been done incorrectly.

> [1] In elementary schools in this country, even when pupils are failing, they are promoted to the next grade, and this practice is called social promotion. [2] An alternative to this approach is retention, which means a child is left back and can't progress to the next grade, although retention also has many negative academic and emotional effects. [3]Therefore, social promotion and retention are both ineffective, and don't enhance students' learning. [4]Consequently, many parents and educators are demanding better services for their children because the real issue is that no one cares if these children are educated because they come from low-income families.

4. What has been done incorrectly in this summary? The writer:

a. did not paraphrase.

b. provided inaccurate information in the summary.

c. provided supporting details in the summary.

d. did not include the title of the passage and a reference to the author.

e. b and d [18]

20

5. Re-read sentence number four and explain what is wrong with it. The passage:

   a. did not state that parents were *demanding* better services.

   b. stated that parents and educators are inept.

   c. did not state that no one cares about low-income children.

   d. a and c. [19]

Read the following summary written about Practice Passage Five, and answer the questions that follow to explain what is incorrect.

> [1] According to the author of "Television Commercials and Obesity among Children," physicians used to believe that viewing television excessively increased obesity among children. [2] A current study has shown that watching television isn't what causes childhood obesity. [3] It is the food advertisements that influence youngsters' eating habits. [4] Advertisers have figured out how to lure children into eating fattening foods when they are little. [5] This new study disproves the "couch potato" effect among obese children.

6. In this summary, the writer:
   a. provides incorrect information.
   b. includes supporting details instead of the main idea.
   c. does not include transition words to connect each thought.
   d. copies the exact words from the passage. [20]

7. Revise the summary and wherever necessary, insert transition words.

   _____

   _____

   _____

   _____ 21

21

Read the following summary written about Practice Passage Four, and answer the questions that follow to explain what is incorrect.

> [1] According to the author of "Advertisements on Tobacco Products," a new law will mandate more obvious health cautions on ads for cigarettes and smokeless tobacco. [2]Therefore, cigarette packages and smokeless tobacco containers must increase the size of their warnings and use tougher language. [3] Currently, the tobacco industry is trying to lure in new customers by not explaining that smokeless tobacco can cause cancer and nicotine addiction. [4] Despite these new laws, many marketing specialists do not believe that the larger warnings will have a considerable influence on consumers.

8. In this summary, the writer:
    a. only discusses one major detail
    b. includes a supporting detail.
    c. uses inappropriate language.
    d. does not paraphrase.
    e. a and c [22]

9. Use the numbers placed before each sentence to specify which sentence should **NOT** be included in the summary.

    a. 1
    b. 2
    c. 3
    d. 4 [23]

Read the following summary written about Practice Passage Three. Then answer the questions that follow to explain what is incorrect.

> [1]Approximately three hundred high-school students participated in a one-day injury prevention program.[2]In addition, the students toured an intensive care unit at a hospital and met young people who had suffered mild brain or spinal cord injuries in car accidents. [3]The results of the survey implied that teenage drivers consistently underestimated driving risks.[4]They believed that most fatal crashes resulted because of car, weather, or highway problems, instead of mistakes in judgment. [5]In contrast, the teenagers who participated in the safety program developed more appropriate insights into dangers on the road. [6]This study indicates that teen drivers should be reminded frequently that poor judgment and inexperience increase the risk of serious injuries and death.

10. What is wrong with the sentence number one? It:

    a. begins the summary with a supporting detail when it states "three hundred students participated in a one-day injury prevention program.

    b. does not introduce the main idea of the passage: Teenagers have more car accidents and driving fatalities than any other age group because they greatly misjudge risky driving situations.

    c. does not mention the title of the passage or the author.

    d. a, b and c [24]

11. What sentence should replace sentence number one?

    a. A recent study determined that adolescents have more deadly car crashes because they underestimate dangerous driving situations, according to the author of "Driving Safety Programs for Teens."

    b. A group of high school students took part in a one-day injury prevention program, according to the author of "Driving Safety Programs for Teens."

    c. According to the author of "Driving Safety Programs for Teens," students visited a hospital to see teens who were seriously injured in car accidents.

    d. The students toured an intensive care unit at a hospital and met young people who had suffered mild brain or spinal cord injuries in car accidents. [25]

12. What is wrong with sentence numbers two, three and four? They:

    a. provide inaccurate information that was not in the article.

    b. are out of order.

    c. do not explain that a survey was taken before the students participated in a program.

    d. b and c [26]

13. It isn't it necessary to include sentence number two because it is:

    a. inaccurate.

    b. a supporting detail.

    c. repetitive

    d. all of these [27]

14. What critical information is missing between sentences numbers five and six? Between these two statements, the writer needs to:

    a. explain why teens need to be reminded of driving safety.

    b. add some statistics to support the main idea.

    c. provide the number of students who participated in this program.

    d. b and c. [28]

15. Read each of the revised summaries, and indicate which one does not contain supporting details and presents the summary in an organized, clear fashion.

a.   A survey among 300 high school students implied that teenage drivers consistently underestimated driving risks, according to the author of "Driving Safety Programs for Teens." After participating in a one-day injury prevention program, the students toured an intensive care unit at a hospital and met young people who had suffered mild brain or spinal cord injuries in car accidents. They believed that most of the fatal crashes resulted because of car, weather, or highway problems, instead of mistakes in judgment. In contrast, the teenagers who participated in the safety program developed more appropriate insights into dangers on the road. This study indicates that teen drivers should be reminded frequently that poor judgment and inexperience increase the risk of serious injuries and death.

b.   A recent study determined that adolescents have more car crashes and deadly accidents because they underestimate dangerous driving situations, according to the author of "Driving Safety Programs for Teens." Before participating in the study, the students completed a survey in which they indicated that they believed most fatal crashes resulted because of car, weather, or highway problems, instead of errors in judgment. In contrast, after the teens took part in a driving safety program, they developed more appropriate insights into dangers on the road, but several weeks after the program this knowledge decreased. Therefore, these results suggest that teen drivers should be reminded frequently that poor judgment and inexperience increase the risk of serious injuries and death. [29]

Read the following summary written about Practice Passage Three. Then answer the questions that follow to explain what is incorrect.

[1]In the passage entitled, "Television Commercials and Obesity among Children," the author claims that for years, doctors have believed that too much time in front of the television increased childhood obesity. [2]However, a recent study has demonstrated that it is not the act looking at a television, but _____. [3]In a recent study, the researchers expected to find that children who watched a lot of television would be overweight. [4]According to this article, doctors realized that the chance of being obese increased when children watched too many fattening food advertisements. [5]Over the years, doctors have developed ways to attract customers and build food loyalty among children when they are little. [6]For many years, they believed that children who watched a lot of television became obese. [7]This study also indicated that children need to participate in more physical activity to prevent obesity.

16. What information needs to be added at the end of sentence number two?

    a.   because children don't exercise enough.
    b.   because children view too many advertisements for fattening foods.
    c.   because their parents don't feed them properly.
    d.   b and c [30]

25

17. If sentence number two is completed accurately, why aren't sentences three and four necessary? They are unnecessary because _____ [31]

18. What is also wrong in sentence numbers four and five? In these sentences, the writer:

   a. states that parents and teachers discovered that commercials caused the weight gain.
   b. should state that the *researchers* determined that commercials caused in the weight gain, *not doctors*.
   c. should state that *advertisers* have developed ways to attract customers and build food loyalty among children when they are little, *not doctors*.
   d. a, b and c
   e. b and c [32]

19. Why is it unnecessary to include sentence number six? It is unnecessary to include sentence number 6 because _____. [33]

20. What is wrong with sentence number seven? It _____. [34]

21. Re-write the summary paragraph so that it is acceptable. [35]

_____
_____
_____
_____
_____
_____
_____
_____
_____
_____

Read the following summary written about Practice Passage Four. Then answer the questions that follow to explain what is incorrect.

---

[1] According to the author of "Advertisements on Tobacco Products," although cigarettes and smokeless tobacco products have health warnings on each package, they appear in tiny print in a small corner. [2]Therefore, according to a new law, the warnings must be larger than before. [3]However, the advertising professors think that even if the warnings are bigger, they will not be effective. [4]However, the larger warnings will not have a significant influence on consumers. [5]In addition, because smoking has decreased, the tobacco industry has begun to use smokeless tobacco to attract new customers, even though these products can cause cancer and nicotine addiction. [6]For these reasons, the new law will require much larger health warnings on packages of cigarettes and smokeless tobacco. [7]The warning must cover the top half of the front and back of each container, and they must make the warning stronger and provide colorful graphics. [8]In response to these new laws, many tobacco companies have started lawsuits because they believe these laws deny them the right to free speech.

---

22. What is done incorrectly in sentence number three? It:
    a. uses incorrect vocabulary.
    b. provides a supporting detail.
    c. is repetitive.
    d. a and b [36]

23. What word is used incorrectly in sentence number three?
    a. However
    b. Advertising
    c. Professors
    d. Effective [37]

24. What word could be used instead of "professors" in sentence three?

    a. experts

    b. executives

    c. authorities

    d. a, b and c [38]

25. In sentence number four, what has been done incorrectly? This sentence:

    a. doesn't paraphrase enough.

    b. uses an transition word of contrast when a transition word of result is required.

    c. is unclear and poorly written.

    d. a, b, and c [39]

26. What transition word should be used instead of "however" in sentence number four?

    a. On the other hand

    b. Therefore

    c. In contrast

    d. Finally [40]

27. Read the following sentence and try to paraphrase the underlined words.

    Therefore, the larger warnings will not have a <u>significant</u> influence on <u>consumers</u>. [41]

    _____

    _____

28. Sentence number seven is problematic because it:

    a. supplies inaccurate information.

    b. is a supporting detail.

    c. is repetitive.

    d. all of these [42]

Answer Key for Chapter One

1. Answer f
2. Answer a
3. Answer c
4. Answer d
5. Answer b
6. Answer c
7. Answer b
8. Answer b
9. Answer b
10. Answer a
11. Answer c
12. Answer f
13. *According to Kurt Wagner in "Distracted: Are you paying $75 an hour sit in class and check Facebook," m*any college instructors are discouraged because of the rise in the number of students who send text messages and check social networks during class. One study suggests that this occurs because many learners have trouble paying attention in class since losing focus is part of human nature. Moreover, the ability of students to concentrate and learn in the classroom varies according to their own individual motivation and also on the pedagogy used by the professor. Finally, the author indicates that when students don't concentrate during class, they waste the money they spend on tuition.
14. Answer d.
15. Answer c
16. Answer c
17. Answer d
18. Answer e
19. Answer d
20. Answer c
21. Answers may vary.
    According to the author of "Television Commercials and Obesity among Children," physicians used to believe that viewing television excessively increased obesity among children. **In contrast, a** current study has shown that watching television isn't what causes childhood obesity. **Conversely,** it is the food advertisements that influence youngsters' eating habits**, because** advertisers have figured out how to lure children into eating their fattening foods when they are little. **Therefore,** this new study disproves the "couch potato" effect among obese children.
22. Answer b
23. Answer c
24. Answer d
25. Answer a
26. Answer d
27. Answer b
28. Answer a
29. Answer b
30. Answer b
31. They repeat information already provided.
32. Answer e
33. it is repetitive.
34. provides information not stated in the passage.
35. In the article entitled, "Television Commercials and Obesity among Children," the author claims that for years, doctors have believed that too much time in front of the television increased childhood obesity. However, a recent study has demonstrated that obesity does not result because children watch too much television, but because they view too many advertisements for fattening foods, which advertisers have designed to attract children and build food loyalty when they are little.
36. Answer a
37. Answer c
38. Answer d
39. Answer b
40. Answer b
41. Therefore, the larger warnings will not have a <u>noteworthy</u> influence on <u>people who use these products</u>.
42. Answer b

Chapter Two

Organizing Your Essay

When the CATW readers grade your paper in addition to your summary, they will evaluate the organization and development of your ideas and your ability to use varied approaches to support your thoughts in your body paragraphs. To achieve these goals, this chapter will explain how to:

- select and state a thesis for your essay;
- create topic sentences;
- compose supporting details;
- integrate information from the passage into your supporting details; and
- write an effective conclusion.

Determining Key Ideas for Discussion

According to the CATW test instructions, you must develop *one* key idea in the reading passage and explain its significance in an essay. If you recall in the previous chapter, key ideas refer to the main idea and the major details in the reading passage. Thus, to determine which point you will discuss in your essay, you should examine the key ideas stated in the summary for the article entitled, "Distracted: Are you paying $75 an hour sit in class and check Facebook." They are as follows:

- Many college instructors are discouraged because of the rise in the number of students who send text messages and use social networks during class.

- One study suggests that these distractions occur because many learners have trouble paying attention in class since losing focus is part of human nature.

- The ability of students to concentrate and learn in the classroom varies according to their own individual motivation and on the pedagogy used by the professor.

- When students don't pay attention during class, they waste the money they spend on tuition.

Selecting One Key Idea for Discussion

Examine the preceding list of key ideas, and circle one, which you can easily discuss in detail in your essay. You may also want to reduce this statement so that you can narrow the focus of your essay. For instance, you might choose the following key idea:

The ability of students to concentrate and learn in the classroom varies according to their own individual motivation and on the pedagogy used by the professor.

Next, narrow down the thesis statement and make certain it is clear so that your essay is easy to organize and compose.

The ability of students to concentrate ~~and learn in the classroom~~ *in class* varies according to their ~~own individual~~ motivation and ~~also on the pedagogy used by~~ the professor*'s pedagogy*.

Finally, turn your thesis statement into a question. For instance, you can create the following question for the above mentioned thesis statement:

Why does the ability of students to concentrate in a class vary according to their motivation and the professor's pedagogy?

Practice Turning Key Ideas into Thesis Statements and Questions

Read the following key idea.

1.   One study suggests that these distractions occur because many learners have trouble paying attention in class since losing focus is part of human nature. [a]

    a.   Narrow down the thesis statement and make certain it is clear so that your essay is easy to organize and compose.

        _____

        _____   1

    b.   Turn the thesis statement into a question.

        _____

        _____   2

2.   When students don't pay attention during class, they waste the money they spend on tuition.

    a.   Narrow down the thesis statement and make certain it is clear so that your essay is easy to organize and compose.

---

[a]   **WARNING:** You MUST clarify the term "these distractions," or else your reader will not know that it describes texting and using social networks in class.

_____

_____ 3

b. Turn the thesis statement into a question.

_____

_____ 4

Drafting the Introduction

To stay focused on this test, you should create an outline to guide and organize you as you draft your CATW essay. The first step is to compose the introduction and summary paragraphs.

1. Introduction Paragraph

   In the first paragraph, which is the introduction paragraph, you should state your thesis as a question.

2. Summary Paragraph

   In the next paragraph, write your summary of the article.

Read the following introduction and summary paragraphs, and pay special attention to how the thesis is introduced by using the thesis question you just created.

Why does the ability of students to concentrate in a class vary according to their motivation and the professor's pedagogy?

According to Kurt Wagner in "Distracted: Are you paying $75 an hour to sit in class and check Facebook," many college instructors are discouraged because of the rise in the number of students who send text messages and check social networks during class. One study suggests that this occurs because many learners have trouble paying attention in class since losing focus is part of human nature. Moreover, the ability of students to concentrate and learn in the classroom varies according to their own individual motivation and on the pedagogy used by the professor. Finally, the author indicates that when students don't pay attention during class, they waste the money they spend on tuition.

---

1. The purpose of the first paragraph is to:

   a. make it longer.

   b. state the thesis (or key idea) of this essay.

32

c. summarize the article in one sentence.

d. none of the above [5]

2. The purpose of the second paragraph is to:

   a. state the thesis.

   b. provide the summary required for the CATW test.

   c. provide supporting details.

   d. none of the above [6]

3. If you don't directly state the thesis you plan discuss, the people who grade the CATW exam will:

   a. think you don't know how to compose a effective thesis statement.

   b. assume you didn't understand the CATW test instructions.

   c. be confused as to what you plan to discuss in your essay.

   d. all of the above [7]

Error Analyses of Introduction Paragraphs

Each of the following introductions and summaries contains problems. Read them and respond to the questions below to determine what is done incorrectly.

> I disagree when college students don't pay attention in class.
>
> According to Kurt Wagner in "Distracted: Are you paying $75 an hour to sit in class and check Facebook," many college instructors are discouraged because of the rise in the number of students who send text messages and check social networks during class. One study suggests that this occurs because many learners have trouble paying attention in class since losing focus is part of human nature. Moreover, the ability of students to concentrate and learn in the classroom varies according to their own individual motivation and on the pedagogy used by the professor. Finally, the author indicates that when students don't pay attention during class, they waste the money they spend on tuition.

4. This first paragraph which states the thesis is unacceptable because:

   a. the writer discusses two key ideas instead of one.

33

b. this essay is not a agree/disagree paper, but one in which you must select one key idea and discuss it.

c. the writer did not follow the CATW test instructions, which direct him/her to discuss one key idea.

d. b, and c [8]

Read the next paragraph taken from the Practice Passage Two about social promotion and retention, and determine what is missing.

> According to the author of the passage, "Social Promotion and Retention," in elementary schools in this country, even when pupils do not learn the required material, they are socially promoted to the next grade. An alternative to this approach is retention, which means a child is left back and can't progress to the next grade. However, this practice also has many negative academic and emotional effects. In fact, it has been reported that both social promotion and retention are ineffective and don't enhance students' learning. Therefore, many parents and educators want schools to offer more personalized approaches.

5. The writer:

a. only provides a summary paragraph.

b. does not include a thesis paragraph, which states the key idea to be discussed.

c. provides repetitive and inaccurate information.

d. does not follow the CATW test instructions.

e. a, b and d [9]

Read the next introduction paragraph about Practice Passage Two on social promotion and retention, and determine what is done incorrectly.

> Does retention result in serious issues that can ruin a child's academic future?
>
> According to the author of the passage, "Social Promotion and Retention," in elementary schools in this country, even though pupils are failing, they are socially promoted to the next grade. An alternative to this approach is retention, which means a child is left back and can't progress to the next grade. However, this approach also has many negative academic and emotional effects. In fact, the Department of Education has reported that both social promotion and retention are ineffective, and don't enhance students' learning. Therefore, many parents and educators want schools to offer more personalized approaches.

6. The writer:

   a. only provides a summary.

   b. never states what idea he/she plans to discuss.

   c. provides repetitive and inaccurate information.

   d. drafted an acceptable introduction. [10]

Writing Effective Topic Sentences

As mentioned previously, the key idea (the main idea or major detail) that you have selected will be the **_thesis_** of your essay, and you will state the thesis in the first paragraph before your summary paragraph. Next, you must decide what you want to discuss in the body paragraphs of your essay. To determine what points to discuss, it is helpful to use your thesis question. For instance, you just created the following question for the above mentioned thesis.

> *Why does the ability of students to concentrate in a class vary according to their motivation and the professor's pedagogy?*

Next, you can develop some points or reasons to write about in each body paragraph by asking and answering the thesis question. Please note: each body paragraph will discuss a combination of the *thesis* and *one specific point or reason, not two reasons or points*. Observe the following example.

Why does the ability of students to concentrate in a class vary according to their motivation and the professor's pedagogy?

1. Many college students have difficulty focusing in class because their instructors spend the entire lesson giving long, boring lectures.

2. Many college students can't concentrate in class because they are not motivated to learn about subjects unrelated to their careers or majors.

3. Many college students are easily distracted during class because they have many personal responsibilities in addition to their college studies.

4. Many college students can't focus in class because they are not yet committed to doing the work necessary to get a college degree.

5. Many college students can't concentrate in class because they are addicted to sending text messages.

Composing Topic Sentences

After selecting the reasons/points you want to discuss, you must compose a **topic sentence** for each body paragraph you will write. Then, you will use these topic sentences as the first sentence in each body paragraph. In fact, each body paragraph should begin with a topic sentence so that your reader knows exactly what point you will discuss and because it will help you stay organized and on topic when you are under the pressure of writing a timed ninety-minute essay.

Each topic sentence should state:

- the thesis (the key idea) of your essay, and
- one point or reason that you will discuss in detail in the body paragraph.

Note: You should *ALWAYS* refer back to the thesis questions and answers that you drafted when you write topic sentences.

For instance in the first body paragraph, your topic sentence could state the following:

                                                            ↓ **point you will discuss**

                                 ↓ **thesis (key idea)**   **in body paragraph one**

Many college students have difficulty focusing in class because their instructors spend the entire class providing long, boring lectures.

The **second body paragraph** should state the **same key idea** and **a second point** that you will discuss in body paragraph two. For instance your topic sentence could state the following:

                                            ↓**point you will discuss**

    ↓ **thesis (key idea)**   **in body paragraph two**

Many college students can't concentrate in class because they are not motivated to learn about subjects unrelated to their careers or majors.

Varying Vocabulary

Please note that although both topic sentences provided the same exact thesis statement, they each used different words to describe the thesis: why college students experience difficulty paying attention in class. Good writers strive to vary their vocabulary by not using the same exact words in each paragraph. Moreover, varying your vocabulary will result in a more enjoyable essay, and it will demonstrate to the CATW readers that you have a strong vocabulary and good command of the English language.

Practice Creating Topic Sentences

1.   Use the previous examples and the thesis question answers to compose a topic sentence. [b]

              ↓ **point you will discuss**

    ↓ **thesis (key idea)**   **in body paragraph three**

_____

_____ 11

2.   Use the previous examples and the thesis question answer to compose your topic sentence.

              ↓ **point you will discuss**

    ↓ **thesis (key idea)**   **in body paragraph four**

_____

_____ 12

---

[b]   It is not always necessary to write three paragraphs, if your first two body paragraphs are well-developed and provide enough information to prove your point.

Error Analyses of Topic Sentences

Each of the following topic sentences has a problem. Read them carefully, and respond to the questions below.

1. I believe this policy can have a serious negative impact on a child.

   In this topic sentence, the writer:

   a. does not directly state the thesis or key idea the writer will discuss in this paragraph.

   b. provides a supporting detail instead of a reason.

   c. doesn't discuss the correct topic.

   d. all of these [13]

2. Social promotion is ineffective because a large percentage of the students that are socially promoted drop out of school.

   In this topic sentence, the writer:

   a. does not write about the assigned topic.

   b. doesn't state the thesis.

   c. uses a statistic/fact, which is a supporting detail.

   d. b and c [14]

3. What would be the most appropriate topic sentence for this supporting detail?

   When underprepared students are socially promoted, a large percentage of these learners tend to drop out of school.

   a. Social promotion is ineffective, whereas retention helps students learn what they missed.

   b. Social promotion doesn't help students develop the skills required to succeed in school.

   c. Social promotion has a serious negative and emotional impact on students.

   d. When social promotion was compared to retention, many of the students impacted by this policy dropped out of high school. [15]

4. The following topic sentence was created for the Practice Passage One entitled, "Married Women Who Work Are Happier." Determine why it is incorrect.

   Married women who work are more satisfied with their marriages.

   This topic sentence:

a. does not mention the thesis or key idea.

b. does not include a reason or a point to be discussed in this body paragraph.

c. provides a thesis or key idea that was not mentioned in the passage. [16]

5. Which of the following is an acceptable topic sentence? (Hint: if it is an example, fact, statistic, definition, cause effect, comparison/contrast, etc., it cannot be a topic sentence.)

a. Many couples don't believe the happiness of their marriage depends on having children because very few childless couples get divorced.

b. Many couples don't believe the happiness of their marriage depends on having children because they place more value their careers.

c. Marital happiness should not depend on whether or not a couple has children. [17]

6. Why can't the following sentence be a topic sentence?

Many couples don't believe the happiness of their marriage depends on having children because very few childless couples get divorced.

_____

_____ [18]

7. Why can't the following sentence be a topic sentence?

Marital happiness should not depend on whether or not a couple has children.

_____

_____ [19]

Outlining the Essay

Once you have developed your thesis paragraph, summary paragraph, and topic sentences, you should create an outline and follow it as you write.

Why do many college students have difficulty concentrating in class?

According to Kurt Wagner in "Distracted: Are you paying $75 an hour to sit in class and check Facebook," many college instructors are discouraged because of the rise in the number of students who send text messages and check social networks during class. One study suggests that this occurs because many learners have trouble paying attention in class since losing focus is part of human nature. Moreover, the ability of students to concentrate and learn in the classroom varies according to their own individual motivation and on the pedagogy used by the professor. Finally, the author indicates that when students don't pay attention during class, they waste the money they spend on tuition.

Many college students have difficulty focusing in class because their instructors spend the entire lesson providing long, boring lectures. _____

_____

Next, many college students can't concentrate in class because they are not motivated to learn about subjects unrelated to their careers or majors. _____

_____

Finally, many college students can't focus in class because they are not yet committed to doing the work necessary to get a college degree. _____

_____ [c]

In conclusion, _____ [d]

Writing the Essay

Now that you have designed a clear, well-organized outline, it is time to write the supporting details for your essay.

---

[c] Once again, it is not always necessary to write three paragraphs, if your first two body paragraphs are well-developed and provide enough information to prove your point well. However, if these body paragraphs contain fewer than six sentences, you should compose a third body paragraph.

[d] Although writing a conclusion has not yet been discussed, it is essential that you include a conclusion paragraph so that the CATW readers realize that you know how to end a composition. Therefore, you should incorporate a conclusion into your outline so that you do not forget to write one.

Warning: Many inexperienced writers create an outline, but fail to use it as a guide when they write. Thus, they end up composing a disorganized off-topic essay, which can result in a failing grade. Therefore, you should always refer to your outline as you compose your essay.

Read the following introduction, and the first body paragraph, which begins with a topic sentence and contains supporting details that all discuss the thesis and the reason/point provided in the topic sentence. In addition, in accordance with the CATW instructions, the writer has also *integrated specific information from the reading passage* into the supporting details.

Why do many college students have difficulty concentrating in class?

According to Kurt Wagner in "Distracted: Are you paying $75 an hour to sit in class and check Facebook," many college instructors are discouraged because of the rise in the number of students who send text messages and check social networks during class. One study suggests that this occurs because many learners have trouble paying attention in class since losing focus is part of human nature. Moreover, the ability of students to concentrate and learn in the classroom varies according to their own individual motivation and on the pedagogy used by the professor. Finally, the author indicates that when students don't pay attention during class, they waste the money they spend on tuition.

Many college students have difficulty focusing in class because their instructors spend the entire lesson presenting long, boring lectures. Last semester when I took a history class, my professor sat at her desk and read aloud from her notes or the textbook. She didn't even try to interact with us. When we tried to ask questions, she would ignore us and just continue to talk. As a result, most students played with their phones and sent text messages, or if they had a laptop, they would log on to Facebook to complain about how boring the class was or to make fun of the instructor. At the end of the term, I heard that more than half the class had failed, and many others were lucky if they received a grade of C or D. In fact, according to the article, 91 % of students admitted to using their phones during college classes to send text messages, even though they understood that this distraction might prevent them from earning good grades. My history class was a perfect example of this dilemma. In contrast, throughout the semester, I tried my best to listen to her lectures and take careful notes, but I frequently caught myself daydreaming and missing important information, even though I never touched my phone during her class. In fact, in the article, Dr. Bounce stated that a student's ability to learn not only depends on their level of motivation, but on the teaching method used by the instructor. Obviously, if this professor had made any attempt to make the presentation of her class more interesting, many students like me would have been able to focus, learn more and earn better grades.

Next, many college students can't concentrate in class because they are not motivated to learn about subjects unrelated to their careers or majors. _____

_____

_____

Finally, many college students can't focus in class because they are not yet committed to doing the work necessary to get a college degree. _____

_____

_____

In conclusion, _____

Body Paragraph Development

Each supporting detail and any information you provide from the reading passage must directly relate to the thesis you're discussing and the specific reason or point you stated in your topic sentence. If your supporting details do not tie into your topic sentence or contain unnecessary information, you'll stray off topic.

The following list suggests several methods used to develop supporting details.

   a. examples or short stories, that are direct and get right to the point;

   b. facts or statistics, but they should be realistic not an exaggeration of reality;

   c. cause/effect relationships;

   d. comparisons or contrasts (similarities and differences);

   e. definitions; and,

   f. appropriate quotes.

Techniques Used to Develop Body Paragraphs

Read the first body paragraph below and note the specific techniques used to develop it.

↓ topic sentence   ↓thesis
Many college students have difficulty focusing in class because their instructors spend
↓point/reason to be discussed in body paragraph   ↓ personal example
the entire lesson presenting long, boring lectures. Last semester when I took a history class,
          ↓ the writer explains cause of the boredom in her class
my professor sat at her desk and read aloud from her notes or the textbook. She didn't even
          ↓the writer provides another reason why she was bored in class
try to interact with us. When we tried to ask questions, she would ignore us and just continue

42

Transition word
↓ **of result**   ↓ **the first effect of the boredom**

to talk. As a result, most students played with their phones and sent text messages, or if they

↓ **the second effect of the boredom in class**

had a laptop, they would log on to Facebook to complain about how boring the class was or

↓**transition word of time**   ↓**third effect of the boredom in class**

to make fun of the instructor. At the end of the term, I heard that more than half the class had

transition
↓**fourth effect of the boredom in class**   ↓ **word**

failed, and many others were lucky if they received a grade of C or D. In fact, according to

↓ **reference to the article**

the article, 91 % of students admitted to using their phones during college classes to send text

notice how the reference to the article directly relates
↓**to the personal example, but isn't repetitive**

messages, even though they understood that this distraction might prevent them from earning

↓ **connects the information from the article**   **Transition word of**
to the personal example   ↓**unexpected result**

good grades. My history class was a perfect example of this dilemma. In contrast, throughout

↓ **second personal example information that differs from the article**

the semester, I tried my best to listen to her lectures and take careful notes, but I frequently

caught myself daydreaming and missing important information, even though I never touched

Transition   **another reference to the article that**
↓**word**   ↓**relates directly to the author's 2ⁿᵈ personal example**

my phone during her class. In fact, in the article, Dr. Bounce stated that a students' ability to

learn not only depends on their level of motivation, but on the teaching method used by the

transition
↓**word of closure**   ↓ **sentence the ends the body paragraph**

instructor. Obviously, if this professor had made any attempt to make the presentation of her

↓**ends paragraph by bringing the reader back to the reason provided in the topic sentence**

class more interesting, many students like me would have been able to focus, learn more and earn
better grades.

Transition Words

As mentioned in Chapter One, transition words are used to create a smooth connection from one
written idea to the next. However, it is important to use the transition word that conveys the
correct meaning. If you don't, your writing will be choppy and disconnected.

Practice Using Transition Words

The chart below specifies some commonly used transition words. The second column provides
the meaning of the transition words. For practice, in the third column, write a **compound
sentence** that uses each transition word(s) correctly. An example is provided.

Transition Words	Meaning	Sentence
However	a contrast or unexpected result	Maria and Marco wanted to spend more time together; however, it was impossible because they both had to work 18 hours a day.
Nevertheless		
In addition		
Therefore		
For instance		
On the other hand		
As a result		
Furthermore		
Finally		
Moreover		
Obviously		
Thus		
Besides		
In contrast		

20

Practice Identifying the Type of Supporting Details Used

Read the next body paragraph, and above each sentence, specify the technique used to introduce the topic sentence and supporting details. Also, specify transition words and point out the details that refer back to specific information provided in the reading passage.

Next, many college students can't concentrate in class because they are not motivated to learn about subjects unrelated to their careers or majors. During my history class, I overheard several students mention that they were nursing majors, so they thought learning history was a waste of their time and money. As a result, while they took lecture notes on their

44

computers, they also played on social networks or sent Instant Messages. By the end of the fifty-minute lecture, some of them were not even taking notes. Thus, as the article stated these students switched between being engaged and non-engaged for less and less time. Consequently, after the midterm exam, when they realized that they were failing the course, they had to make the difficult choice of dropping the class and losing the tuition they had paid, or failing the course and risking not being admitted to the college's competitive nursing program. Thus, as the article indicated, these students wasted their time and money on tuition because they were not motivated to pay attention during a history course since they failed to see its connection to their major. [21]

Practice Writing Supporting Details

With a partner, read each topic sentence and write appropriate supporting details by using the techniques you just observed in the previous paragraphs.

Finally, many college students can't focus in class because they are not yet committed to doing the work necessary to get a college degree. _____

_____

_____

_____

_____

_____

_____

_____

Error Analyses of Supporting Details

Each body paragraph below is taken from a practice CATW essay. Read each carefully and examine the supporting details to determine what has been done incorrectly. After you analyze each paragraph, respond to the questions that follow.

Many advertising professionals do not think that larger health warnings on cigarette packages will stop people from buying cigarettes because most consumers are already addicted and cannot stop smoking. Research has demonstrated that some people become addicted to the nicotine in cigarettes as soon as they begin to smoke. Thus, when they go to a store to purchase cigarettes, they're looking for a fix to satisfy their addiction. As a result, they will not bother reading the health warnings, regardless of their size. They just want a smoke, and they want it immediately.

1. In this body paragraph, the writer:

   a. does not discuss the reason provided in the topic sentence.
   b. does not provide enough supporting details.
   c. does not refer back to the article.
   d. b and c. [22]

2. Add some appropriate supporting details and references to the article so that this body paragraph is well developed.

   Many advertising professionals do not think that larger health warnings on cigarette packages will stop people from buying cigarettes because most consumers are already addicted and can't stop smoking. Research has demonstrated that some people become addicted to the nicotine in cigarettes as soon as they begin to smoke. Thus, when they purchase cigarettes, they're looking for a fix to satisfy their addiction. As a result, they will not bother reading the health warnings, regardless of their size. They just want a smoke, and they want it immediately. _____

   _____

   _____

   _____

   _____

Read the following body paragraph and answer the questions that follow.

Many advertising professionals do not think that larger health warnings will stop people from buying cigarettes because young people smoke to fit in with their peers and rarely worry about their health. Most teenagers believe they are invincible and that nothing can happen to them. So, when they want to fit in with their friends who smoke, they smoke, too. When they purchase cigarettes, they only think about their image among their peers, not their health. Consequently, I doubt that they will bother to read the health warnings no matter how big they are. When my boyfriend was 15, he started to smoke, even though he knew he could develop health problems, because he had witnessed his grandfather's death from lung cancer after the man had smoked for 30 years. Despite this vivid visual and emotional experience, he took up smoking because he wanted to be cool. In fact, research has indicated that when most teens take up smoking, it is because of peer pressure. Clearly, peer pressure is the reason teens take up smoking.

3. In the last two sentences of this body paragraph, the writer:

   a. strays off the topic.
   b. repeats the same information.
   c. contradicts his/her previous statements.
   d. b and c. [24]

4. What is wrong with the information specified in the last two sentences?

   a. The last two sentences provide research and a concluding sentence that do not relate to the topic sentence.
   b. The writer doesn't demonstrate how the young man who saw his grandfather die from lung cancer would have been affected by larger health warnings on cigarette packages.
   c. All of the above. [25]

5. Can you revise the last three sentences so that they directly tie into the topic?

_____

_____

_____

_____ 26

6. For this exercise, refer to the reading passage entitled, "Driving Safety Programs for Teens" and answer the questions that follow.

    Research has indicated that the majority of teens have had very little practice in stressful driving situations. Consequently, as the article stated they aren't adept at predicting and preventing potential problems, so they get involved in far more accidents than experienced drivers who have these skills. For instance, a month after Igor got his license as he was driving on the highway, a red car in the left lane started to swerve. Since my friend didn't realize that this behavior signaled potential trouble, he accelerated and tried to pass this red car, but the red car turned into his lane and crashed into his car. In contrast, in a similar situation, my father tapped on his horn to alert the other driver and prevent an accident. In fact, a recent study indicated that because teens frequently underestimate dangerous driving situations, they end up in life-threatening crashes. Clearly, Igor and many other teens don't have enough experience to identify and deal with hazards on the road.

7. What is missing from this paragraph?

_____ 27

8. A topic sentence for this paragraph could read as follows:

   a. Most adolescent drivers are inexperienced, so they are extremely dangerous on the road.
   b. Many teenagers drive so recklessly that they can't anticipate problems on the highway.
   c. Although teen drivers may have quicker reflexes, they frequently lack the experience and judgment to negotiate dangerous driving situations.
   d. Teen drivers should be forced to drive with adult supervision for a year before they are permitted to drive by themselves. [28]

48

After you read the following body paragraph about the passage entitled, "No Junk Food in Schools," determine what has been done incorrectly in the supporting details.

[1]Banning sugary and fried foods from schools won't prevent childhood obesity because children develop bad eating habits at home. [2]Many people think that feeding children healthy meals at school will teach them to eat well. [3]However, children develop their eating habits at a very young age at home. [4]My cousin's next-door neighbor is an excellent example. [5]He lives in California, and we have known his child since he was born. [6]In California, junk food has already been banned at the schools. [7]When this child was less than two years old, he was already drinking gallons of sugary soda from his baby bottle, and [8]because both his parents worked, they routinely purchased fast food for his dinner. [9]As a result, this child survived on a steady diet of cheeseburgers, french fries, cakes, soda, etc. [10]Therefore, when he entered kindergarten, he was already very heavy, and [11]even though his school only served nutritious meals, he disliked those meals and refused to eat them. [12]Instead, his parents packed him a lunch, which contained ring dings, potato chips, soda, and candy. [13]It is obvious that the healthy food served at his school had no impact because his poor eating habits had already been established at home. [14] Besides, many elementary-school teachers have noticed that even when unhealthy foods are prohibited, many children continue to sneak them in because that is what they are used to eating. [15]Undoubtedly, this new law will not influence children's eating habits because they are deeply rooted by the time they enter school.

9. This body paragraph is problematic because:

    a. the supporting details are redundant.
    b. there isn't enough body paragraph development.
    c. several of supporting details are long, boring and unnecessary.
    d. all of the above [29]

10. The sentences that are inappropriate are numbers:

    a. seven, eight and nine.

49

    b. four, five and six.

    c. six, seven and eight.

    d. fourteen. [30]

11. The sentences that are inappropriate because:

    a. they are repetitive.

    b. they provide needless, uninteresting information.

    c. they don't directly relate to the topic.

    d. b and c [31]

12. How should this paragraph be corrected?

    a. Sentences four, five and six should be placed in another body paragraph.

    b. Sentences four, five and six should be deleted from the body paragraph.

    c. Sentence seven should be revised so that this child is first mentioned without a lot of unnecessary, boring information.

    d. b and c [32]

13. Can you revise this paragraph below?

_____

_____

_____

_____

_____

_____

_____

_____

Read the following body paragraph written about the passage in Chapter Three entitled, "Going on a Diet? Start Paying in Cash." Then answer the questions that follow to determine what has been done incorrectly in the supporting details.

[1]The most interesting point this article reveals is that when people use credit cards to shop, they tend to spend more because credit card users don't experience the pain of payment. [2]However, according to the article, when consumers make purchases with their credit cards, they are more likely to buy unnecessary, unhealthy products because they don't experience the negative feeling of watching their cash leave their wallets. [3]However, customers who make purchases using cash spend less because they monitor their money as they see it leave their hands. [4]For instance, when my mother shops for food, she pays with her credit card, and spends a lot more than when she uses cash. [5]In contrast, my grandmother only uses cash in the supermarket, so she spends less than my mother does. [6]According to the article, this occurs because the pain of payment diminishes impulsive responses, and thus reduces the purchase of vice products. [7]This indicates that paying with credit or debit cards stimulates costumers to spend more, whereas cash makes consumers behave more conservatively.

14. What word is used incorrectly in sentence number 2, and why is this incorrect?

_____

_____

15. In sentence number 2, the transition word *however* should be:

a. deleted

b. replaced with Moreover

c. replaced with On the other hand

d. b and c [35]

16. What is wrong with sentences numbers and 4 and 5? These two sentences:

    a. contradict each other.

    b. don't discuss the point stated in the topic sentence.

    c. basically repeat the same information provided in sentences 2 and 3.

    d. are acceptable and should not be revised. [36]

17. Can you revise sentences 4 and 5 so that they provide new information that is not repetitive?

    _____

    _____

    _____
                                                                          [37]
    _____

18. Which word is spelled incorrectly in sentence number 7?

    a. stimulates

    b. costumers

    c. consumers

    d. conservatively [38]

19. What is the correct spelling of this word?
                                                          [39]
    _____

The Conclusion Paragraph

After you have drafted your body paragraphs, be certain to include your conclusion so that you finish your essay in a clear, thought-provoking manner. Read the following conclusion and answer the questions that below them.

Clearly, both the college professors and their students are responsible for the lack of focus in their classes because some instructors make no attempt to captivate their learners' attention while many students are unenthused about learning.

1. What is the purpose of a conclusion?

   _____ 40

2. How does this writer conclude this topic?

   _____ 41

3. Does this conclusion repeat any information that was in the essay word for word?

   _____ 42

4. Can you draft your own conclusion for this essay?

   _____

   _____

   _____

   _____ 43

The Entire Essay

The next page provides you with a complete view of the essay used in book so that you can visualize what a finished CATW essay should look like.

Why do many college students have difficulty concentrating in class?

According to Kurt Wagner in "Distracted: Are you paying $75 an hour to sit in class and check Facebook," many college instructors are discouraged because of the rise in the number of students who send text messages and check social networks during class. One study suggests that this occurs because many learners have trouble paying attention in class since losing focus is part of human nature. Moreover, the ability of students to concentrate and learn in the classroom varies according to their own individual motivation and on the pedagogy used by the professor. Finally, the author indicates that when students don't pay attention during class, they waste the money they spend on tuition.

Many college students have difficulty focusing in class because their instructors spend the entire lesson presenting long, boring lectures. Last semester when I took a history class, my professor sat at her desk and read aloud from her notes or the textbook. She didn't even try to interact with us. When we tried to ask questions, she would ignore us and just continue to talk. As a result, most students played with their phones and sent text messages, or if they had a laptop, they would log on to Facebook to complain about how boring the class was or to make fun of the instructor. At the end of the term, I heard that more than half the class had failed, and many others were lucky if they received a grade of C or D. In fact, according to the article, 91 % of students admitted to using their phones during college classes to send text messages, even though they understood that this distraction might prevent them from earning good grades. My history class was a perfect example of this dilemma. In contrast, throughout the semester, I tried my best to listen to her lectures and take careful notes, but I frequently caught myself daydreaming and missing important information, even though I never touched my phone during her class. In fact, in the article, Dr. Bounce stated that a student's ability to learn not only depends on their level of motivation, but on the teaching method used by the instructor. Obviously, if this professor had made any attempt to make the presentation of her class more interesting, many students like me would have been able to focus, learn more and earn better grades.

Next, many college students can't concentrate in class because they are not motivated to learn about subjects unrelated to their careers or majors. During my history class, I overheard several students mention that they were nursing majors, so they thought learning history was a waste of their time and money. As a result, while they took lecture notes on their computers, they also played on social networks or sent Instant Messages. By the end of the fifty-minute lecture, some of them were not even taking notes. Thus, as the article stated these students switched between being engaged and non-engaged for less and less time. Consequently, after the midterm exam, when they realized that they were failing the course, they had to make the difficult choice of dropping the class and losing the tuition they had paid, or failing the course and risking not being admitted to the college's competitive nursing program. Thus, as the article indicated, these students wasted their time and money on tuition because they were not motivated to pay attention during a history course since they failed to see its connection to their major.

Clearly, both the college professors and their students are responsible for the lack of focus in their classes because some instructors make not attempt to captivate their learners' attention while many students are unenthused about learning.

Error Analyses of Conclusion Paragraphs

Each of the following conclusions is problematic. Read them carefully and respond to the questions that follow.

[1] It is obvious that both students and teachers are responsible for the lack of attention in many college classrooms. [2] It is sad that many students can't pay attention for more than ten to twenty minutes in a class. [3] In fact, research has demonstrated that students switch between being engaged and non-engaged in ever-shortening cycles throughout a class. [4] Therefore, it is time for professors to make their classes more interesting, and for students to learn to concentrate better, or else this country will produce poorly educated people in the years to come.

1. In this conclusion, the writer:

    a. does not discuss the thesis or key idea of the essay.

    b. includes supporting details.

    c. strays off topic.

    d. a and c [44]

2. Which sentence(s) in this conclusion should be omitted because they are supporting details?

    a. one and four

    b. one and two

    c. two and three

    d. three and four [45]

3. What type of supporting detail is sentence number two?

    a. definition

    b. short story

    c. cause/effect relationship

    d. fact and/or statistic [46]

4. What type of supporting detail is sentence number three?

    a. a fact

b. a short story

c. a quote

d. a definition [47]

5. Can you revise the conclusion so that it does not include supporting details?

_____

_____ [48]

Read the following conclusion for the passage entitled, "Advertisements on Tobacco Products," and answer the questions that follow.

It is obvious that people will still take up smoking even after watching a close friend or relative suffer a long, painful death from cigarette smoking. My cousin took up smoking even after he watched his father die from cancer, so no matter what laws are enacted, people will continue to take up smoking.

6. In this conclusion, the writer:

a. does not conclude the topic of the essay.

b. includes supporting details.

c. strays off topic.

d. a, b, and c [49]

7. Can you revise this conclusion so that it is effective?

_____

_____

_____

_____ [50]

Your Turn to Practice Writing a CATW Essay

Use the summary you created for Reading Passage Two, entitled "Social Promotion and Retention" to specify the key ideas in the passage below.

1. _____

2. _____

3. _____

4. _____

5. _____

Selecting One Key Idea for Discussion

Examine the preceding list, and circle one key idea that you can easily write about it in detail in your essay. Then jot it down the following two lines. This key idea will be the thesis of your essay.

_____

_____

After you select the thesis (or key idea) you plan to write about, if it is necessary, reduce or narrow down the point so that it is easier to write about.

_____

_____

Creating a Thesis Question

Next, you should turn your thesis statement into a question.

_____

_____ ?

Stating your Thesis and Writing a Summary

State your thesis question in the first paragraph. In the second paragraph, write your summary about social promotion and retention.

_____

_____

_____

_____

_____

_____

_____

_____

_____

_____

_____

Using the Thesis Question to Brainstorm Ideas for the Body Paragraphs

To develop some points or reasons to discuss in each body paragraph, respond to your thesis question below. Please note: each body paragraph will discuss a combination of the _thesis_ (one key idea) and _one specific point or reason, not two reasons or points_. Your thesis should not include supporting details.

1. _____

2. _____

3. _____

4. _____

Writing Topic Sentences

After you have created a thesis paragraph and a summary paragraph, it is time to write your topic sentences. As you may recall, each topic sentence should state the **thesis** (key idea), and **one reason/point that you will discuss** in each body paragraph, but it should **not include supporting details**. [e]

Topic Sentence One:

_____

_____

Topic Sentence Two:

_____

_____

Topic Sentence Three:

_____

_____

Conclusion

_____

_____

_____

Writing Your Essay

Now that you've drafted an outline for your essay, use it to compose your CATW essay. When you're drafting your supporting details, be certain to refer back to this chapter for guidance and suggestions.

Good Luck!

---

[e] Please note: it is only necessary to compose two body paragraphs if they are **well developed**. However, if you realize your body paragraphs are too short, you should write a third body paragraph.

Answer Key for Chapter Two

1. Many college students get distracted in class by text messages and social networks because it is human nature to lose focus.

2. Why does human nature cause many college students to get distracted by text messages and social networks?

3. When college students get sidetracked by technological distractions in class, they waste their time and money.

4. Why don't college students realize that getting sidetracked by technological distractions in class will result in wasting their time and money?

5. Answer b

6. Answer b

7. Answer d

8. Answer d

9. Answer e

10. Answer d

11. ↓ point you will discuss in body paragraph three   ↓ thesis (key idea)

    As a result of having many personal responsibilities in addition to their college studies, many students can't focus well in class.

12.   ↓ point you will discuss

            ↓ thesis (key idea)   in body paragraph three

    Many college students can't pay attention in class because they are not yet committed to doing the work required to get a college degree.

13. Answer a

14. Answer c

15. Answer b

16. Answer b

17. Answer b

18. This statement is a fact, and facts are used as supporting details, but **not** in topic sentences.

19. This sentence states the writer's opinion, not a reason why married couples believe the success of their marriage does or does not depend on having children.

20. Nevertheless	Unexpected result or contrast	Answers will vary.
In addition	Additional information	Answers will vary.
Therefore	A result	Answers will vary.
For instance	An example	Answers will vary.
On the other hand	An unexpected result or contrast	Answers will vary.
As a result	A consequence	Answers will vary.
Furthermore	Additional information	Answers will vary.
Finally	The last point	Answers will vary.
Moreover	Additional information	Answers will vary.
Obviously	Clearly	Answers will vary.
Thus	Result or conclusion	Answers will vary.
Besides	Additional information	Answers will vary.
In contrast	A difference	Answers will vary.

21. **Transition word**
    to connect body 1
    ↓and body 2   **topic sentence**   **↓thesis or key idea**

    Next, many college students can't concentrate in class because they are not motivated to learn

    ↓point to be discussed in the body paragraph   **↓personal example**

    about subjects unrelated to their careers or majors. During my history class, I overheard

    ↓tying the personal example into the point being discussed in this body paragraph

    several students mention that they were nursing majors, so they thought learning history was

                                   ↓transition of

    ↓cause   **consequence**

    a waste of their time and money. As a result, while they took lecture notes on their

↓**first effect**   ↓**transition of time**

computers, they also played on social networks or sent Instant Messages. By the end of the
                                                                    transition
↓**second effect**   ↓ **of result**

fifty-minute lecture, some of them were not even taking notes. Thus, as the article stated
                              ↓**reference to the article**

these students switched between being engaged and non-engaged for less and less time.
Transition of   ↓**continuation of personal**
↓ **consequence**   **example**   ↓**cause**

Consequently, after the midterm exam, when they realized that they were failing the course,
        ↓**effect 1**

they had to make the difficult choice of dropping the class and losing the tuition they had
        ↓**effect 2**

paid, or failing the course and risking not being admitted to the college's competitive nursing
                  transition
        ↓**word of result**   ↓**reference to the article**

program. Thus, as the article indicated these students wasted their time and money on tuition
        ↓**ends paragraph by returning to the reason provided in the topic sentence**

because they were not motivated to pay attention during a history course since they failed to
see its connection to their major.

22   Answer d

23   Answers can vary.

    Many advertising professionals do not think that larger health warnings on cigarette packages will stop people from buying cigarettes because most consumers are already addicted and can't stop smoking. Research has demonstrated that some people become addicted to the nicotine in cigarettes as soon as they begin to smoke. Thus, when they purchase cigarettes, they're looking for a fix to satisfy their addiction. As a result, as the article stated, they will not bother reading the health warnings, regardless of their size or colorful graphics. In fact, even if the warning took up half of the package, it wouldn't stop my brother from smoking. When my brother gets off from work, the first thing he wants to do is smoke. So, he races to the store, buys a pack of cigarettes, tears off the cellophane, and lights up. He doesn't even look at the container. He just needs to satisfy his craving for nicotine. My brother is only one example of many smokers; therefore, as the article stated, this law will have little to no impact on cigarette consumers.

24   Answer a

25   Answer c

26   Answers will vary.

    Despite this vivid, visual, and emotional experience, he took up smoking anyway because he wanted to be cool. ***Therefore, if seeing someone he loved die from the effects of smoking didn't influence him, a warning on a package won't either.*** In fact, research has indicated that when most teens take up smoking it is because of peer pressure***, so larger health warnings and colorful graphics will not influence them much***. Clearly, peer pressure is the reason teens take up smoking, ***so health warning on cigarette packages will not stop teens from smoking.***

27   Answer: This paragraph is missing a topic sentence.

28   Answer c

29   Answer c

30   Answer b

31   Answer d

32   Answer d

33   Banning sugary and fried foods from schools won't prevent childhood obesity because children develop bad eating habits at home.[1] Many people think that feeding children healthy meals at school will teach them to eat well.[2] However, children develop their eating habits at a very young age at home.[3] ~~My cousin's next door neighbor is an excellent example.~~[4] ~~He lives in California, and we have known his child since he was born.~~[5] ~~In California, junk food has already been banned at his school~~[6]. When ~~this child~~ *Paolo* was less than two years old, he was already drinking gallons of sugary soda from his baby bottle[7], and because both his parents worked, they routinely purchased fast food for his dinner.[8] As a result, this child survived on a steady diet of cheeseburgers, french fries, cakes, soda, etc.[9] Therefore, when he entered kindergarten, he was already very

heavy, [10] and even though his school only served nutritious meals, he disliked them and refused to eat them. [11] Instead, his parents packed him a lunch, which contained ring dings, potato chips, soda, and candy. [12] It is obvious that the healthy food served at his school had no impact because his poor eating habits had already been established at home. [13] Besides, many elementary school-teachers have noticed that even when unhealthy foods are prohibited, many children continue to sneak in them in because that is what they are used to eating. [14] Undoubtedly, this new law will not influence children's eating habits because they are deeply rooted by the time they enter school.

34 Although no contrast is being made, the writer uses the transition word of contrast, however.

35 Answer a

36 Answer c

37 Answers may vary. For instance, when my mother shops for food and pays in cash, she usually spends about $150 a week and rarely purchases junk food. However, when she pays with her credit card, she spends over $210 because she picks up additional goodies such as candy, cookies, potato chips, and expensive body care products that she really doesn't need.

38 Answer is b

39 customers

40 The purpose of a conclusion is to provide the reader an ending that offers a satisfying sense of completion.

41 The writer finishes this composition by emphasizing the fact that both teachers and students are responsible for the distractions in college classrooms.

42 No, no repetition should be avoided because it is boring and uncreative.

43 Answers will vary.

44 Answer b

45 Answer c

46 Answer d

47 Answer a

48 It is obvious that both students and teachers are responsible for the lack of attention in many college classrooms. Therefore, it is time for professors to make their classes more interesting, and for students to learn to concentrate better, or else this country will produce poorly educated people in the years to come.

49 Answer d

50 Answers will vary. It is obvious that people will still take up smoking even if they know it is dangerous. Therefore, warnings on tobacco products will have very little impact on consumers.

Chapter Three

Additional Practice Reading Passages

The purpose of this chapter is to provide additional reading passages so that you can practice the techniques you've learned in preparation for the CATW test.

Passage One

Disruptions: Life's Too Short for So Much E-Mail [1]

by Nick Bilton

Just thinking about my e-mail in-box makes me sad. This month alone, I received over 6,000 e-mails. That doesn't include spam, notifications or daily deals, either. With all those messages, I have no desire to respond to even a fraction of them.

It's not that I'm so popular. Last year, Royal Pingdom, which monitors Internet usage, said that in 2010, 107 trillion e-mails were sent. A report this year from the Radicati Group, a market research firm, found that in 2011, there were 3.1 billion active e-mail accounts in the world. The report noted that, on average, corporate employees sent and received 105 e-mails a day.

Sure, some of those e-mails are important. But 105 a day? All of this has led me to believe that something is terribly wrong with e-mail. What's more, I don't believe it can be fixed. I've tried everything. Priority mail, filters, more filters, filters within filters, away messages, third-party e-mail tools. None of these supposed solutions work.

Last year, I decided to try to reach In-box Zero, the Zen-like state of a consistently empty in-box. I spent countless hours one evening replying to neglected messages. I woke up the next morning to find that most of my replies had received replies, and so, once again, my in-box was brimming. It all felt like one big practical joke.

Meanwhile, all of this e-mail could be increasing our stress. A research report issued this year by the University of California, Irvine, found that people who did not look at e-mail regularly at work were less stressed and more productive than others. Gloria Mark, an

---

informatics professor who studies the effects of e-mail and multitasking in the workplace and is a co-author of the study, said, "One person in our e-mail study told us after: I let the sound of the bell and pop-ups rule my life."

I recently sent an e-mail to a teenage cousin who responded with a text message. I responded again through e-mail, and this time she answered with Facebook Messenger. She was obviously seeing the e-mails but kept choosing a more concise way to reply. Later, we talked about the exchanges, and she explained that she saw e-mail as something for "old people." Since technology hasn't solved the problem it has created with e-mail, it looks as if some younger people might come up with their own answer - not to use e-mail at all.

So I'm taking a cue from them. I'll look at my e-mail as it comes in. Maybe I'll respond with a text, Google Chat, Twitter or Facebook message. But chances are, as with many messages sent via Facebook or Twitter, I won't need to respond at all.

Passage Two

Cell Phones and Driving

Recent laws have legislated that drivers must use hands-free cell phones if they are operating a car. Nevertheless, many people contend that when a driver talks on a cell phone, it is the same as conversing with a passenger in the car. However, researchers have discovered that cell phone conversations are far more distracting to a driver than a conversation with a passenger. The difference is that most passengers stop talking when they notice problematic driving conditions. Moreover, passengers in a car can provide additional input to warn the driver when an exit is approaching or another driver is behaving unpredictably.

To compare the effects of drivers' engaging in cell phone conversations to a driver chatting with a passenger in a car, about 100 drivers were placed in a simulator. They were instructed to drive several miles on a highway and to pull off at a specific exit. One set of drivers participated in this experiment while they were talking to a friend in the car, whereas the other drivers chatted on hands-free cell phones.

Almost all the drivers who were talking to a passenger completed the task successfully; in addition, some of their passengers assisted the drivers by providing feedback. However, fifty percent of the cell phone users failed to notice the exit and drove by it. The authors of this experiment concluded that when drivers use hands-free cell phones, their driving skills are reduced so much that their driving ability is equal to a driver under the influence of alcohol.

Passage Three

Study: Facebook Users Are Friendlier [2]

Facebook, it turns out, isn't just a waste of time. People who use it have more close friends, get more social support and report being more politically engaged than those who aren't, according to a new national study on Americans and social networks. The report comes as Facebook, Twitter and even the buttoned-up, career-oriented LinkedIn continue to ingrain themselves in our daily lives and change the way we interact with friends, co-workers and long-lost high school buddies.

Released yesterday by the Pew Internet and American Life Project, the report also found that Facebook users are more trusting than their non-networked counterparts. When accounting for all other factors - such as age, education level or race - Facebook users were 43 percent more likely than other Internet users to say that "most people can be trusted."

Compared with people who don't use the Internet at all, Facebook users were three times more trusting. When all else is equal, people who use Facebook also have 9 percent more close ties in their overall social network than other Internet users. This backs an earlier report from Pew that, contrary to studies done earlier in the decade, the Internet is not linked to social isolation. Rather, it can lead to larger, more diverse social networks.

The survey was conducted among 2,255 adults from Oct. 20 to Nov. 28, 2010. The margin of error is plus or minus 2.3 percentage points for the fun sample.

Passage Four

Advantages of Community Colleges

Community colleges offer several advantages over four-year colleges. First, most charge less tuition than four-year colleges, so that these institutions attract students from low-income

---

[2] Used with permission of The Associated Press Copyright © 2012. All rights reserved.

backgrounds. Many community college students are also the first ones in their families to attend college, or they are non-traditional students. Although some have just graduated from high school, many others are adults who have returned to school for a career change or to develop new skills.

Second, community colleges have special importance to minorities. Currently one-half of all African-American and Hispanic undergraduates in the United States attend community colleges. In addition, many community colleges provide special English as a Second Language (ESL) programs for students whose first language is not English. These programs intend to develop ESL learners' language proficiency so that they can succeed in college-level courses.

Finally, the primary focus of faculty at community colleges is teaching. In contrast, at four-year colleges, the faculty's priority is to conduct research and to publish their findings. Thus, although community college professors tend to teach more classes, their focus is on discovering and implementing pedagogies that reap the most success among community college *the statagy of education* learners. Thus, students in community colleges tend to develop closer, more productive relationships with their instructors.

Passage Five

An E-Book Fan, Missing the Smell of Paper and Glue [3]

By Nick Bilton

This past weekend, while visiting New York on a short work-related trip, I was reminded of how much I miss printed books. I set out to wander the city aimlessly, and I came across a small, old corner bookstore along the cobbled streets of the West Village.

I immediately stopped, looking at the dozens of books in the shop's window, and it quickly occurred to me that I had not been into a physical bookstore in months. Instead, I now shop in online digital bookstores and read novels on my Kindle or iPad.

So I went inside, pushing open the large wooden door, which creaked like a prop borrowed from a horror-movie set. As I closed it behind me, a bell on the top dinged. A girl behind the

---

66

counter looked up, smiled and went back to reading her book. A few customers quietly milled about. There were, of course, books stacked everywhere. Thick ones. Thin ones. Large and small. I immediately felt a sense of nostalgia that I haven't felt in a long time. The scent of physical books — the paper, the ink, the glue — can conjure up memories of a summer day spent reading on a beach, a fall afternoon in a coffee shop, or an overstuffed chair by a fireplace as rain patters on a windowsill.

IPads and Kindles, in comparison, don't necessarily smell like anything. For those of us who have switched to e-readers, the e-book shopping experience, while immediate and painless, is about as sentimental as a trip to the family doctor. There are no creaking doors, or bells that announce your arrival so someone can smile at you as you walk inside. There isn't even anything distinctive in the size, shape or feel of the book you're buying.

There is no nostalgia in online book shopping.

Before the days of the iPad, one of my favorite Saturday afternoon activities was to go to a local bookstore, wander the aisles picking out books I might like, then plop myself down in the corner to examine the first few pages of each, deciding what to buy.

As I tiptoed through the bookstore in New York, I thought about doing just that. But then I thought about having to lug those volumes back to San Francisco. I was reminded of the impracticality of these physical books. While they were beautiful, I remembered that I wouldn't be able to search for specific words in them. Or share passages with friends, simply by copying and pasting, on Twitter and Facebook. Or that I can't stuff 500 different books in my backpack without breaking my back.

I ended up walking out of the bookstore without buying anything.

Yes, I miss physical books. I miss bookstores, too. I miss them a lot. I only hope that someone figures out how to give their digital counterparts a little more feeling.

Passage Six

College Students Behaving Badly [4]

Many people associate property crime and other delinquent behaviors with low social status and a lack of education. But new research has identified a surprising risk factor for bad behavior — college.

Men who attend college are more likely to commit property crimes during their college years than their non-college-attending peers, according to research to be presented at the annual meeting of the American Sociological Association in Boston this weekend.

During adolescence, the prospect of attending college was positive. The researchers found that college-bound youth were less likely to be involved in criminal activity and substance use during adolescence than kids who weren't headed for college.

But college attendance appears to trigger some surprising changes. When male students enrolled in four-year universities, levels of drinking, property theft and unstructured socializing with friends increased and surpassed rates for their less-educated male peers.

The reason appears to be that kids who don't go to college simply have to grow up more quickly. College enrollment allows for a lifestyle that essentially extends the adolescent period, said Patrick M. Seffrin, the study's primary investigator and a graduate student and research assistant in the department of sociology and the Center for Family and Demographic Research at Bowling Green State University.

College delays entry into adult roles like marriage, parenting and full-time work. Instead, college students have lots of unstructured social time. Other studies have linked unstructured socializing or "hanging out" with higher levels of delinquency and risk taking.

"College attendance is commonly associated with self-improvement and upward mobility," Mr. Seffrin said in a press release. "Yet this research suggests that college may actually encourage, rather than deter, social deviance and risk-taking."

---

[4] From *The New York Times*, July 31 © 2008 The New York Times. All rights reserved. Used by permission and protected by the Copyright Laws of the United States. The printing, copying, redistribution, or retransmission of this Content without express written permission is prohibited.

Passage Seven

Texting While Walking [5]

by Casey Neistat

Navigating the sidewalks of New York City can be as challenging as any rushing sport, like football or rugby. But when your opponents are walking while text messaging, their field of view is impaired, and this can render a three-block walk to Starbucks somewhere between infuriating and life-threatening.

While there's little current data about the number of people injured while texting, more than 1,000 pedestrians visited emergency rooms in 2008 after they were injured while using a cellphone to talk or text. That had doubled each year since 2006, according to a study conducted by Ohio State University.

I wanted to make a movie about this issue for years, and got started after a discussion with my friend Benny Safdie on the proper, courteous way to text while walking. By mastering the etiquette of texting, I hope we can gain more control over our increasingly electronic lives. Let's stop acting like hollowed-out zombies, with BlackBerrys and iPhones replacing eye contact, handshakes and face-to-face conversations. It's time to live once again in the present and simply be where we are.

Passage Eight

Is College for Everyone?

For years, children have been told that a college degree will result in better employment, higher incomes, and more prestige. But, is a college education for everyone? According to the Department of Education, only fifty percent of the people who enter college earn a degree. The statistics are even worse for minority students, especially those who graduated in the lowest

---

quarter of their high school class. As a result, some educators are proposing that the weaker learners not attend college because they might benefit more from vocational programs.

Moreover, the need for some careers such as teachers and accountants are expected to decline. In contrast, employment opportunities in the fields of home health aides, customer service, and clerical workers will increase. Training for these occupations is completed through vocational programs; however, this training has diminished as a result of the national movement for improved educational standards. Consequently, few pupils are guided into vocational fields.

One concern about tracking students into vocational programs is that this approach may lower the expectations of weaker, poorer students and may result in educational redlining. This means many minority learners will be discouraged from attending college if their teachers fail to recognize and/or develop their potential. As a result, many underprivileged teens will never receive exposure to an environment that might help them mature academically and professionally.

Passage Nine

No Junk Food in Schools!

In an attempt to reduce childhood obesity, legislation has been proposed to forbid junk food from being served in schools. These new regulations would ban sugary and fried foods from school cafeterias and vending machines nationwide. As a result, schools will only serve nutritious foods so that children can make healthy choices. Several cities and states have already passed laws to remove certain drinks and snacks from schools' vending machines, and they are proposing modifications to school lunch menus, too.

Presently, most school lunches are quite unhealthy. They consist of hot dogs, pepperoni pizza, cheeseburgers, french fries, and sugary flavored milks. Many of these meals contain more than half a day's worth of sodium and fat. However, this new law would require schools to offer more fruits, vegetables, whole grains, and low-fat milks. It is hoped the introduction of nutritious, plant-based foods at a young age will establish healthy eating habits and reduce the children's risk of developing Type 2 diabetes, cancer, strokes, and heart disease.

Although the National Parent Teachers Association and other health groups support this law, others are unenthusiastic. Civil rights activists believe these new laws interfere with parental rights because what a child eats is a private family matter. In addition, the American Beverage Association contends that this law is ineffective in managing weight problems because obesity is a complex issue that results from lack of exercise, excessive calories, fast food, and heredity. Moreover, many parents object to this legislation because they believe overeating is rooted in patterns established at home, not school. Therefore, they claim that serving healthy food at school will not prevent childhood obesity.

Passage Ten

Spoiled Children

Many parents spoil their children by giving into their every whim, even though this treatment can have serious negative consequences. "To spoil" means to damage or ruin something. Therefore, spoiled children become injured psychologically so that they are unable to negotiate the challenges of adult life.

When parents are too indulging or generous with their children, they prevent these youngsters from learning how to achieve goals by themselves. As a result, they miss the opportunity to grow into independent people who appreciate the value of hard work and success. Instead, they develop a demanding sense of entitlement, and rarely consider the needs of others. Consequently, spoiled children typically experience difficulties at work and in relationships since they have acquired little or no respect for order, fairness, and honesty. Worse yet, spoiled children fail to develop good self-esteem because they haven't enjoyed the opportunity of exploring both success and failure as they mature.

Parents can determine if their children are spoiled by examining their ability to cooperate and respect order. If they are unable to work with others and must always have their own way, chances are they are spoiled. However, when parents refuse to honor such demands, children learn to toil patiently toward a goal, and become self-sufficient, supportive adults. Although it is difficult for parents to sit quietly in the background while a child struggles, it is far more rewarding when parents watch their children achieve difficult goals on their own.

Passage Eleven [6]

College Athletes and Academics

Many people believe that participation in collegiate sports leads to lower grades. It is thought that time dedicated to athletics is time taken away from academics. After all, college athletes are consumed by hours of daily practice, and frequently have to miss class for competitions. Thus, many conclude that if student athletes had more time to devote to their schoolwork, they would achieve more academic success. However, the reality is that participation in sports is linked to higher academic achievement because hectic schedules force athletes to develop better time-management skills.

Although the average college student has many hours of free time, college athletes must manage their time carefully. This typically means they have to plan homework and studying into their daily routine. In contrast, most college students enjoy less structured schedules, and therefore can delay the completion of assignments, figuring they will eventually get to them. Thus, their work often remains incomplete or fragmented because they dedicate less effort than necessary to earn good grades.

Moreover, college athletes face regulations from the National Collegiate Athletic Association, and are required to maintain a minimum GPA to compete. In fact, some athletes risk losing their scholarships if they do not meet the minimum criteria. This warning motivates many athletes to attack their schoolwork with the same vigor they exhibit on the playing field. On the other hand, regular students do not face these challenges, and therefore may not feel pressured to maintain their grades. Finally, college athletes are often given access to free tutoring and other services that regular students don't enjoy.

Although at first glance it may appear that the average college student has a distinct advantage over student athletes, this assumption is inaccurate. College athletes are forced into a structured, disciplined lifestyle and receive additional support, all of which produces a recipe for academic success.

---

[6] Written by Theresa E. Rush

Passage Twelve

Spoiled Brats!

Generation Y refers to young people born between 1982 and 2002. They used to be described as a gifted and positive group, but more recently many employers, teachers, and mental-health professionals have portrayed them as malcontents and complainers. Many psychologists believe they have developed a strong sense of entitlement because they were spoiled by parents and teachers who told them how great they were, in order to build their self-esteem.

Numerous college professors have complained about this generation's demanding, constant e-mail contact, their text messaging during class, and their use of their parents to challenge bad grades, which were frequently deserved. As they've entered adulthood, countless books have described how uncontrollable they are at work because of their cell-phones, Instant Messages, and iPods. In addition, many cannot accept feedback and criticism.

Recent college graduates make this story even worse. Even though they are entering a job market that has been destroyed by the worst economy in years, they will not work weekends or overtime, and they reject respectable job offers because the work doesn't match their exaggerated self-images. Moreover, although many of those who are employed are unhappy, they never question their attitude or performance. Instead, they truly believe that some employer will observe their greatness and award them a dream job.

Many believe these young people are headed for a major fall because of their unrealistic overconfidence at a time when many adults are struggling to maintain jobs.

Passage Thirteen

What You've Never Had, You Never Miss:

Canadian Couple who Won $11.2m in the Lottery Gives It ALL away to Charity [7]

by Daily Mail Reporter

---

[7] Daily Mail / Solo Syndication

A Canadian couple who won $11.2million on the lottery have given it all away to friends, charities and hospitals. Allen and Violet Large, both in their 70s, said their good fortune earlier this year had been a 'big headache' and they had decided against going on a spending spree. 'What you've never had, you never miss,' Violet, 78, told the Toronto Star. She and Allen, 75, eventually decided it was better to give than receive and were totally at ease with handing over the money.

Married for 36 years, the pair retired in 1983 for a quieter life. Allen had worked as a welder for 30 years and Violet had been employed by a number of confectionery and cosmetic firms. 'We were pretty well set, not millionaires, but comfortable,' said Allen of the couple's financial set-up before their lottery win in July. At the time Violet was undergoing treatment for cancer and the pair feared being taken advantage of by 'crooked people'.

'That money that we won was nothing,' Allen told the Toronto Star. 'We have each other.' Hospitals and charities in Nova Scotia, were among the lucky recipients of the Larges' windfall.

After taking care of their families, the couple then gave donations to a long list of groups they had decided to help, including their local fire department, churches and cemeteries, the Red Cross, the Salvation Army. The hospitals where Violet underwent her treatment and organizations that fight cancer, Alzheimer's and diabetes, also benefited from the couple's largesse.

The Larges have not disclosed how much they gave to each organization but said they are humbled and thankful for the phone calls and letters of gratitude they have received. 'It made us feel good,' said Violet. 'And there's so much good being done with that money.

'We're the lucky ones,' she added. 'I have no complaints.'

Passage Fourteen

Why Must I Take These Courses?

When freshmen enter college, they are often required to take courses that do not relate to their majors. But, what college students don't realize is that the goal of a college education is to prepare a person for many aspects of life. Thus, many colleges require students to complete a variety of courses unrelated to their majors.

Even though high schools dedicate much time to algebra, geometry and trigonometry, these subjects are not always applicable to real-life situations. However, because of the computer age, we are flooded with statistics and must understand what these numbers mean, because advertisers and politicians are very skilled at manipulating data. Thus, an educated person needs to decipher many numerical puzzles.

A course or two in finance is also essential to make informed investment choices. Many Americans have no idea how to manage their money responsibly, so they get sucked into poor investments. A recent survey indicated that many college students don't truly know what stocks and bonds are, nor do they understand the risks these investments pose. However, many of those surveyed believed that stocks would make them rich. Therefore, finance courses are critical and can help people make wise choices.

Educated folks also need to comprehend why people behave the way they do, so a course or two in psychology is helpful. In addition, in today's global economy, many college graduates will interact with people from all over the world, so they also need to understand the way a person's culture impacts his/her behavior and thinking. When we can put ourselves in the shoes of another person, we can deal with him/her more effectively and prevent misunderstandings.

A college education should not just provide a skill, but it should prepare people to negotiate the diverse challenges encountered in modern life.

Passage Fifteen

Hearing Loss among Young People

Within the last five years, it has been determined that one out of five teenagers has suffered a small amount of hearing loss. Hearing loss has increased by almost 20 percent among the adolescent population. Consequently, approximately 6.5 million teenagers suffer from hearing loss issues. Although most hearing loss is minimal, these teens are not able to perceive slight sounds such as a whisper. Say something very low.

Many hearing specialists blame this problem on the high volume adolescents use when they listen to their ipods and MP3 players. Moreover, a study conducted in Australia connected the use of personal listening devices with a 70 percent greater risk of hearing loss.

Even though prolonged exposure to loud noise is harmful to the hearing, these results do not mean that teens cannot enjoy their ipods or MP3 players anymore, but that they should play them at a lower volume. Some experts have suggested that laws should be enacted to limit the number of decibels that these devices can project because most teenagers don't truly believe they can cause hearing loss. In fact, one study revealed that the average college student listened to music at 85 decibels or louder, which is equivalent to listening to a deafening noise non-stop for hours.

Even though many other generations have enjoyed loud music, today youngsters play their music for longer periods of time, almost twice as much as their parents' generation did. Moreover, because devices such as CD players provided a much shorter battery life and limited storage capacity, people who used these devices obtained more limited listening experiences. Therefore, there were fewer opportunities to overload their hearing.

Passage Sixteen

Is Multitasking Productive?

New research has indicated that humans are not skilled at multitasking. Multitasking refers to the simultaneous use of several different media, such as watching television, surfing the Internet, playing video games, text messaging, and reading or writing e-mails at the same time. Thus, multitasking requires people to switch their attention from task to task rapidly. However, scientists contend that the human brain is not wired to perform two tasks simultaneously. According to Earl Miller, a professor of neuroscience at MIT, humans cannot focus on more than one activity at a time because when the brain attempts to process two tasks at once, this demand creates a conflict that causes interference between the two activities. For instance, if a person is speaking on the telephone and answering an e-mail, these two activities require verbal communication and written words, but trying to produce both types of output at the same time results in a clash between the two.

To test this theory, Daniel Weissman and other researchers at the University of Michigan used an MRI scanner to photograph multitaskers' brains as they performed different activities concurrently. The researchers discovered that even simple tasks could overwhelm the brain if a subject tries to perform more than one at a time. For instance, if a woman is looking for two cars, one red and the other black, she must continually switch between the two colors in her mind. However, after she performs this task many times, she will become confused, overwhelmed and unproductive. In fact, recent studies indicated that multitasking reduces productivity by 20 to 40 percent.

Moreover, Russell Poldrack, a psychology professor at the University of California, has determined that multitasking negatively impacts learning. If a person learns while multitasking, that learning is less flexible and more difficult to retrieve. As a result, when students send text messages while they are in a classroom, they reduce their ability to learn.

Passage Seventeen

Moving Often Impacts Children

For years, parents, teachers and psychologists have noticed that youngsters who move repeatedly do not perform well in school, and they often develop behavioral problems. However, more recent studies have indicated that when children relocate frequently, the emotional impact from these relocations influences them for the rest of their lives.

First, frequent relocations negatively impact the academic performance of children. In fact, the more they relocate, the more their educational achievement is at risk. In addition, children who move more than three times before eighth grade are at the greatest risk of dropping out of school.

Children who move repeatedly experience difficulty establishing quality relationships. One young woman stated that as a child, her father was transferred across the country every couple of years. As a result, she had no real close friendships or people with whom she could share childhood memories. As an adult, she still has difficulty making friends. This woman's claim is supported by recent research, which reported that the more frequently people move as children, the more likely they are to describe a lack of well-being and happiness. Worse yet, these folks tend to die at a younger age.

However, this research also pointed out that moving typically affects people with certain personality types. Introverted, shy, nervous people displayed the most negative effects. On the other hand, outgoing people were less affected.

Moreover, children's reactions vary according to the reasons for moving. For instance, children with parents in the military report fewer problems because the military eases the adjustment, and these children enter schools with other military children who have also been relocated. In contrast, when a husband relocates his family because of a job, if his wife responds negatively, her reaction will influence their children. It was also noted that when a move results because of a divorce, the children may respond negatively to the breakup and a reduction in income.

However, researchers and psychologists believe that the consequences of moving are much more complex, and need to be examined more carefully before generalizations can be made.

Passage Eighteen

How to Study Effectively

Scientists have shown that a few simple methods can improve how much people learn when they study. Although these findings have been available for years, most educators don't encourage their use.

One important discovery demonstrated that it is not wise to always study in the same place. Traditionally, when students study, they've been told to locate a quiet spot and to sit silently. However, research has demonstrated that moving from room to room actually improves retention. One study revealed that college students required to memorize a list of vocabulary words in two different rooms performed much better than those who memorized the words in the same room. Other investigations have replicated these results using different subject matter.

Research has also shown that the human brain is capable of making subtle connections between what is being learned and the background in which this learning occurs. If the brain makes different associations with the same course content, this seems to provide the mind more connections through the body's central nervous system. That is if the background in which the studying occurs is mixed, the knowledge becomes easier to recall.

Next, instead of memorizing history notes for an hour, a person might dedicate half an hour to two different subjects because the variation creates a deeper impression on the brain. Interestingly enough, this technique is already used in the fields of music and athletics. For instance, when musicians practice, they usually include a combination of several different pieces, and most athletes employ workouts that contain many diverse exercises. These findings demonstrate that studying different subjects during a single period of time enriches the learning experience.

Passage Nineteen

Going on a Diet? Start Paying in Cash [8]

Paying with credit or debit cards makes people more likely to make impulsive, unhealthy food purchases, according to a new study in The Journal of Consumer Research.

Previous research has found that paying with credit can encourage people to spend more money because physically handing over a dollar bill increases the so-called "pain of payment," which takes away from the pleasure of consumption.

There is a piggy joke to be made here somewhere. It turns out paying with a card can also make consumers likely to spend more money on "bad" things in particular, like junk food.

"When consumers encounter vice products — such as cookies, cakes and pies — the emotive imagery and associated desire trigger impulsive purchase decisions," the authors write. But "pain of payment can curb the impulsive responses and thus reduce the purchase of such vice products."

In part of their study, the authors looked at the shopping behavior of a random sample of 1,000 single-member households who normally shop at chain stores. The authors looked at what these households purchased over a six-month period on each visit to the store, and how they paid for their items. Most of the households switched between card and cash payments on different trips (but the researchers did not randomly assign one form of payment versus another, so there may be some other lurking variables at play).

In this analysis, consumers were significantly more likely to purchase unhealthy foods like cakes and cookies when using a credit or debit card. Interestingly, consumers who shopped with larger baskets were also "more susceptible to impulsive purchase of unhealthy products," the authors found. The date of the shopping trip also made a difference:

Consumers shopping on weekends are less likely to be impulsive. This could be because of the shopping list effect: weekend shopping trips tend to be based on shopping lists, and therefore purchases on such trips are less susceptible to impulsive urges.

The researchers also performed several other experiments, including one in which undergraduate and graduate students simulated a shopping trip on a computer. Students were told they would be paying via cash or card, and even though no money actually changed hands in this imaginary purchase, the card condition was again associated with less healthy purchases.

The authors argue that their work has important implications for public health and policy:

In the popular press as well as in academic publications, the growing obesity problem and its economic consequences have been attributed to consumers' failures to control impulsive urges (Ubel 2009). Further, researchers have identified several factors that make impulse control a challenging goal for consumers. Given this background, the finding that at least some consumers might be able to curb their impulsive urges by paying in cash is of substantive importance.

The paper is by Manoj Thomas of Cornell University, Kalpesh Kaushik Desai of the State University of New York, Binghamton, and Satheeshkumar Seenivasan of the State University of New York, Buffalo.

Passage Twenty

Achieving a Healthful Digital Diet [9]

Think of the Internet and other digital technology as food. Limit the intake of empty digital calories, and do not consume too much over all. That is the advice of experts who study children's use of media and who have some tips for parents and children on how to use technology in more healthful ways.

Michael Levine, executive director of the Joan Ganz Cooney Center, which studies media and learning, said parents should take the time to assess whether a Web site or game had clear educational value. Then, he suggested, tip the balance so that 50 percent of a child's computer time is spent on activities that teach. "The primary use of technology by young people is for entertainment," he said. "There needs to be a more balanced diet."

Vicky Rideout, a researcher who has overseen studies on media and health for the Kaiser Family Foundation, said it was crucial to limit multitasking and entertainment while studying. "Don't have the instant-messaging function open. Don't have Facebook open," she said. "Put that challenge out to the kids."

Some of the expert advice focuses on the example set by parents. "What kind of role model are you?" asked Liz Perle, editor in chief of Common Sense Media, which helps families navigate a media-saturated world. "Are you constantly on your BlackBerry, play online games regularly — are you addicted to Facebook, too?"

Ms. Perle urged parents of younger children not to constantly entertain them with screens, like giving them the iPhone to quiet them in a restaurant. And older children should be given basic phones for talking and texting, not smartphones that can be loaded with applications. Eventually, Ms. Perle said, older children must take responsibility. She suggested they ask questions like those asked by people with addictions: "Who is in control? Me, or the technology? Is the game calling the shots.

Chapter Four

Language Use on the CATW

One of the scores on the CATW test will evaluate your ability to use language effectively. This means you will lose points if you:

- can only write very simple sentences;
- have a limited vocabulary or use words inappropriately; and,
- are unable to express your ideas clearly.

In another domain, you will lose points for grammar, usage, and mechanics. Thus, you must demonstrate the ability to employ the conventions of standard American English. This means you should minimize errors in:

- grammar,

- punctuation, and

- spelling.

Therefore, the intent of this chapter is to review some grammatical and lexical skills to heighten your awareness of common errors that developmental students make, so that you can minimize these issues and pass this exam.

Independent Clauses

1. An independent clause, which is also called a main clause, is a ***complete sentence*** that makes sense by itself.

   e.g.   Smoking cigarettes is unhealthy.
   Many people own cell phones.
   Teenage drivers underestimate their driving ability.

2. A sentence that contains two main clauses is a ***compound sentence***, but compound sentences can contain *only **two** independent clauses.*

3. When a sentence contains *two main clauses*, they are connected with a comma and a conjunction.

(correct →) Today couples don't marry until they are more mature, **and** they also
          don't have children immediately.

4.   The following is a list of conjunctions used to connect two main clauses. But, you must be careful to use the conjunction that expresses the correct meaning.

Conjunction	Meaning	Example
For	a reason	Identity theft can happen to anyone, **for** no one is exempt from this white-collar crime.
And	additional information	The child saw many television ads for sugary cereals, and he insisted his mother buy them.
But	a contrast or unexpected information	Community colleges offer two-year degrees, **but** four-year institutions provide bachelor degrees.
Yet	a contrast or unexpected information	She arrived early for the graduation ceremony, **yet** she still couldn't find a parking space.
Or	a choice	The driver had the choice to use a hands-free cell phone, **or** he could risk receiving a ticket and points on his license.
Nor	negative choice	The child didn't want a hot dog, **nor** did he want a piece of pizza.
So	a result	The salesman needed to speak to customers when he was driving, **so** he purchased a hands-free cell phone set.

5.   Two sentences cannot be separated by a comma. If they are, you have created a *comma splice,* as in the following example.

↓ **comma splice**

(incorrect →) Today couples don't marry until they are more mature, they also don't
          have children immediately.

6.   Two sentences cannot be pushed together. This is called a *run-on sentence*.

↓ **run-on sentence**

(incorrect →) Today couples don't marry until they are more mature they also don't
          have children immediately.

Conjunctive Adverbs and the Semi-Colon

In formal writing, two sentences can be connected with a conjunctive adverb and a semi-colon.

Select the list that contains conjunctive adverbs.

    a. and, but, so, yet, or, nor, for

    b. because, although, even though, before, after

    c. furthermore, moreover, additionally, therefore, however

    d. b and c [1]

Observe how the following compound sentences use conjunctive adjectives to connect them.

    a. The student missed ten classes; therefore, he failed his history course.

    b. The woman witnessed the crime; however, she was afraid to testify in court.

    c. The judge fined the girl; in addition, he ordered her to perform community service for six months.

Write the rule for using conjunctive adverbs to connect two main clauses.

    first   second

    main clause + _____ + _____ + _____ + main clause [2]

Observe what occurs in the following examples when a conjunctive adverb begins a sentence.

    a. The student missed ten classes, so his teacher failed him. Therefore, the student must repeat the course.

    b. The woman witnessed the crime, but she would not testify in court. Consequently, the criminal was not convicted.

    c. The police officer and a witness testified that teenage girl ran a stop sign, so the judge found her guilty. Thus, the young woman had to pay a fine and perform community service for six months.

When the conjunctive adverb is the first word of a sentence, a _____ must follow it. [3]

Warning:

Occasionally, you may be tempted to begin a sentence with the conjunctions *and* or *but*. However, in formal written English, it is better to avoid this practice. Instead, you can begin the sentence with a conjunctive adverb such as additionally, moreover, however, etc.

Using Conjunctive Adverbs to Connect Main Clauses

Conjunctive Adverbs include the following words:

additionally,	in addition,	furthermore,	moreover,	however,
nevertheless,	nonetheless,	besides,	indeed,	thus,
in contrast,	hence,	therefore,	consequently,	as a result,

In formal writing, conjunctive adverbs can be used to connect two main clauses by using the following rule.

e.g.   The police arrested a suspect**; however,** he had an alibi.

The professor had explained the math problem clearly**; therefore,** the students understood it well.

Using Conjunctive Adverbs to Convey the Correct Meaning

Read the following sentences and observe a mistake in the use of the conjunctive adverbs. Then, answer the questions that follow them.

   a.   Lucia planned on visiting her homeland; *therefore*, she cancelled her trip.

   b.   The college was open; *moreover*, many students were absent because of the snow.

In these sentences, the writer used a conjunctive adverb:

   a.   with the correct meaning.

   b.   with the incorrect meaning.

   c.   instead of a conjunction.

   d.   none of these [4]

Warning: When you write, be certain to use the conjunctive adverb that states the intended meaning. The following chart specifies the meaning of these words.

Meaning of Conjunctive Adverbs

Review the following chart to clarify the precise meaning of some commonly *misused* conjunctive adverbs.

To provide **additional** information, use:

in addition	moreover	furthermore	additionally	besides

To provide an **unexpected result** or a **contrast**, use:

however	in contrast	nevertheless	conversely	nonetheless

To demonstrate a **result** or **consequence**, use:

therefore	hence	consequently	as a result	as a consequence
thus				

Error Analysis

Read the following composition and edit it for:

- comma splices, run-on sentences,
- errors in the connection of main and reduced clauses,
- errors in use of conjunctive adverbs, and
- errors in use of conjunctions and conjunctive adverbs that convey the correct meaning.

When I was in college, I worked part time as a bank teller, I also took sixteen credits in college. Although this job didn't pay well, I think it was my favorite job because it was fun and convenient.

The bank that I worked at was located only three blocks from my apartment, however I was able to walk to work, I never had to wait for a bus or pay carfare, and the trip to work only took five minutes. In contrast, when I worked at a mall, I had to take a bus I sometimes waited thirty minutes just for the bus to arrive. Then, if the bus had no room for passengers, I had to wait for the next bus. Additionally, it took me an hour just to get to the mall.

On the other hand, I liked this job because a lot of young people worked at the bank. Moreover, I made lots of new friends. On weekends, after we finished work, we would go out to the movies or have something to eat. Additionally, when I worked at the mall, I didn't make any friends. The people were nice; besides, we had nothing in common. In fact, most of the employees were married adults with families. Therefore, the job at the mall didn't provide any social outlets, but the days seemed endless.

However, the work I did at the bank was interesting, too, we had to interact with the public politely and effectively, even if the customers were not courteous to us. In contrast, we had to be careful not make any mistakes with the money we handled, we had to "prove up" at the end of the day to verify that we hadn't made any errors. For a college student, these demands seemed overwhelming, and they taught me how to function in the business world.

Clearly, working at the bank assisted me in developing many financial, social and business skills; on the other hand, it also permitted me to enjoy meeting new people.

Dependent Adverbial Clauses

1. Adverbial clauses are dependent clauses that cannot stand alone because they are not sentences. They begin with **DANGER WORDS** such as *because, if, when, since, as soon as*, etc. Because they are not complete sentences, dependent clauses do not make sense by themselves. Adverbial clauses must be connected to a main clause. When an adverbial clause is not connected to a main clause, it is a **fragment**. Examine the following examples.

                      ↓**danger**
                      word   ↓ **Fragment**
(incorrect →)   When pupils do not learn the required material.

              ↓ **Dependent clause**   ↓ **Main Clause**
(correct →)   When pupils do not learn the required material, they are promoted to the next grade.

2. A **DANGER WORD** is not a conjunction, so you do NOT place a comma after a danger word. The comma is placed between the dependent adverbial clause and the main clause. Also, because the danger word carries the meaning that connects the dependent clause to the main clause, you do not need to insert a conjunction.

                    ↓**no comma**   ↓**no conjunction**
(incorrect →)   Even though, pupils are failing, ~~but~~ they are promoted to the next grade.

(correct →)   Even though pupils are failing, they are promoted to the next grade.

3. A complex sentence can contain several dependent adverbial clauses, as long as the sentence makes sense and isn't too difficult to comprehend. Observe the number of adverbial clauses in the following sentence.

   ↓**adverbial clause**   ↓**main clause**
Since they have limited incomes and a lot of debt, it is advantageous for them to
                  ↓**adverbial clause**   ↓**adverbial clause**
pay off these loans before they take on the responsibility of a child because they
                       ↓**adverbial clause.**
will be financially secure when they have a family.

Warning: Some writers mix up the word order when they create adverbial clauses by providing a subject + a danger word + pronoun + a verb as in the following example.

(incorrect →) My sister when she was in New York, she visited her children.

(correct →)   When my sister ~~when she~~ was in New York, she visited her children.

The following is a list of commonly used danger words and phrases:

after	although	despite	even if
before	even though	so that	provided that
during	because	such that	as long as
when	every time	in order to	since
until	whenever	whereas	if
while	inasmuch as	wherever	the first time that
though	once	even when	whether
especially	especially when	as soon as	as if
instead of	especially since	because of	in spite of

Practice Exercise

Read the following paragraphs and edit them for

- comma splices,
- run-on sentences,
- fragments, and
- mistakes in punctuation.

1. Many couples postpone having children. In order to make certain that their marriage will endure. Although, children are a blessing. They can add a lot of additional conflicts in a relationship. Moreover, since, modern marriages require a lot of reinforcement to survive, many couples must also learn to negotiate their problems. Before, they decide to introduce a new life into the picture. My cousin when she got married, she decided to wait a few years to have a baby. During this time, she realized that she and her husband were not compatible, so they agreed to a divorce. If they'd had a child. The divorce would have been more complicated.

2. Even though, teen drivers have better reflexes than adults, but many studies have demonstrated that they misjudge hazardous driving situations. Moreover, when teenage drivers engage in distracting activities while they drive. They are more likely to end up in accidents. For instance, while driving, some teens text message their friends, whereas others put on make-up or play with the radio. Many recent studies have proven that even if, a teen driver is cautious, he/she is more likely to have an accident than an experienced adult driver.

3. Because, I came from another country and English was my second language, I didn't read and write well the first year I was in high school. Even though I failed most of my courses, but they promoted me to the next grade.

4. In my country, if students fail, They get left back. Because the teachers believe that the students need to master the material before they move to the next level, I think this policy works better than social promotion.

5. One day, my teacher asked me to read a sentence for her. When I stood up to read the sentence, nothing came out of my mouth; I couldn't speak. Worse yet, as I stood there with my mouth open, everyone in the class began to laugh. This was extremely upsetting, Because I was new in this school and had no friends.

6. When parents experience stress and they sometimes take it out on their child, Because the child is unable to retaliate.

7. This city has mass transit everywhere. Such as buses, trains and taxi cabs. Sometimes two buses and a train all stop at the same corner, it is very easy to get around the city in other cities residents must own a car.

8. My grandfather had heart trouble, the doctors in my country couldn't help him. He came to New York City, the doctors performed heart surgery. So that now he is fine. This city has many famous medical centers. Such as New York Hospital, North Shore University Hospital, and Columbia Presbyterian Medical Center.

9. When I was in first grade, even though, other children played outside on Saturdays, but I had to remain inside and read books with my father. Because he was determined that I would not have to repeat a grade.

10. In the old days, women didn't have the same rights that men have. When they got married and had children. Women were expected to stay home this has changed now. It doesn't mean that their families aren't important, it means they can maintain two important jobs instead of one.

Verb Tenses

The present tense is used to express facts and habitual, routine behavior. Many writers make frequent errors in subject-verb agreement, and they confuse the present tense with the past and present progressive tenses. When you mix up or misuse these tenses, this is viewed as a low-level error, and it suggests you are not ready for college-level writing assignments. To clarify these issues, you will review these tenses to understand the distinction between the two.

The Present Tense

1. The present tense is used to express habitual, everyday actions.

I take the bus to school everyday.	We eat pizza on Fridays
You brush your teeth before bed at night.	He loves old movies.
She hates writing.	They like to sing in the choir.
It rains in California a lot.	

2. In the present tense, when the subject is he, she or it, the letter *s* is added to the simple form of the verb. For all other subjects, use the simple form of the verb.

I <u>love</u> old movies.	We <u>love</u> to read mysteries.
You <u>love</u> to dance.	
She <u>loves</u> ice cream.	
He <u>loves</u> to sing.	They <u>bark</u> a lot.
It <u>begs</u> for food.	Dogs <u>beg</u> for food.

Warning: Instead of using the correct present-tense form, some writers use a verb + ing (barking, loving, talking), but this is incorrect. It is not a tense in English, and it should not be used in standard American English.

e.g. (incorrect →) Margarita <u>singing</u> in the choir at her church.

(correct →) Margarita <u>sings</u> in the choir at her church.

Non-Count Nouns and the Present Tense

Count nouns describe people, places or things that can be counted such as dogs, cats, pens, houses, etc. On the other hand, non-count nouns refer to objects or concepts that cannot be counted such as coffee, juice, hair, beauty, information, etc. When you are writing, it is important to remember that in the present tense, non-count nouns must agree with the subject pronoun *it* (the third person singular) as in the following examples.

e.g.   Sugar taste**s** sweet.

The information **is** inaccurate.

Hatred cause**s** wars.

Warning: Non-count nouns are *never* **pluralized** in English.

e.g.   Their information~~s are~~ is not reliable.

Uncontrolled anger~~s~~ get<u>s</u> people in trouble.

Gerunds and the Present Tense

1. A gerund is a verbal noun that ends in *ing* such as singing, dancing.

91

2. A gerund can be used as the subject of a sentence. When it is the subject, the present tense verb agrees with the third person singular. It should be noted that many writers are tempted to make the verb agree with the phrase that follows the gerund; however, this is incorrect. Observe the following examples.

                    ↓ **modifying**
        ↓ **subject**   **phrase**   ↓ **verb**
a.   Smoking two packs of cigarettes a day is very unhealthy.
                  ↓**modifying**
       ↓ **subject**   **phrase**   ↓**verb**
b.   Reading murder mysteries relaxes me.

Indefinite Pronouns and the Present Tense

Indefinite pronouns refer to words such as everyone, someone, no one, nobody, somebody, everybody, etc. Indefinite pronouns must agree with the verb in the third person singular as demonstrated below.

         indefinite
         pronoun ↓   ↓ **verb**
a.   Everybody loves to eat pizza.

         indefinite
         pronoun ↓   ↓**verb**
b.   No one wants to clean my house.

Practice Exercise

Read the following sentences, and edit for errors in the use of the present tense.

1.   Not everyone have a lot of money.

2.   A friend of mine she don't smoke cigarettes.

3.   Financial aid only pay a small percentage of a student's tuition if the student's parents not make a lot of money.

4.   Every person need to feel important.

5.   Being a single parent mean I don't have much time to socialize because I have to focus on my child.

6.   This problem is happen to me many times.

7.   My sister don't work, so when she go shopping, if an item isn't on sale, she doesn't purchased it because she can't afford it.

8.   My other sister is works, so she is buy whatever she wants.

9.   My neighbor doesn't work. She stay home with her son, but she and her husband are always argue about money because they can't pay their bills.

Practice in Context

Read the following paragraphs and determine if the underlined verb uses the present tense correctly. If it is incorrect, edit it.

Many people thinks that when a driver talking on a cell phone, it is the same as conversing with a passenger in the car. However, a recent study showed cell phone conversations sidetracks drivers more than conversations with people in a car. In addition, when drivers uses hands-free cell phones, their driving get so bad that they operate the vehicle like someone who is drunk. I am agree that driving and talking on a cell phones are extremely dangerous.

If a person chatting on a telephone while he/she is driving, this discussion force the driver to focus on the conversation. As a result, the driver don't pay attention to the road, and can easily miss important signals about impending dangerous situations. In fact several studies have demonstrated that these conversations making drivers react slowly. My sister hit a man on a bicycle because she didn't see him in her rear view mirror because she was too busy talking on her cell phone. Now everyone in the family have to worry about a lawsuit, and she must live with the guilt of having injured a person. In contrast, I never talking on a cell phone, because I know I can't pay careful attention.

Clearly, conversing on cell phones while driving distract the driver and can seriously injure innocent people.

The Present Progressive Tense

The present progressive tense is used to express an activity that is actively **in progress**.

I am writing a book right now.   We are listening to the professor.

You are practicing for the CATW test.

He is text messaging his friends.

She is talking on the phone at the moment.   They are drafting an essay.

The dog is barking at the mailman.

The present progressive is formed by using the following rule.

	Present		participle
Subject +	tense of to be (am, is, are)	+	participle of the verb (walking, talking)

e.g   I   am   talking to my aunt on the phone.

What common mistake has the writer made in these sentences?

Maria running to school.

Amed and Sana talking on the phone.

The writer has:

a.   used the past progressive tense.

b.   used the wrong tense.

c.   omitted (left out) the auxiliary verb to be (am, is, or are).

d.   none of these.   [5]

Practice Exercise

Complete each of the following sentences with either the present or the present progressive tense by observing signal words that suggest if an event is a fact, a habit, or is occurring at the moment.

1.   When a person (drive) _____ a car and (talk) _____ on a cell phone at the same time, research has indicated that the driver's ability to concentrate (be) _____ similar to that of a person who (be) _____ under the influence of alcohol.

2.   When teenagers (drive) _____ a car and they (have) _____ several other adolescent passengers in the vehicle, these drivers (be) _____more

94

likely to get distracted. When my teenage son (operate) _____ my vehicle with five of his friends, these friends (create) _____ a distraction.

3.   When a police officer (see) _____ a person who (drive) _____ and (talk) _____ on a cell phone, the officer should pull this person over and give him/her a ticket because this person (be) _____ dangerous.

4.   When drivers (chat) _____ on cell phones, while they (wait) _____ at a red light when the light (turn) _____ green, these drivers frequently (not notice) _____ the green light, so that they (fail) _____ to proceed through the intersection before the light (turn) _____ red again. As a result, the cars that (wait) _____ behind the cell phone user are forced to miss the green light and must wait for it to change again.

The Past Tense

1.   The past tense is used to express an event that has already occurred and is completed. Observe the **boldfaced** past tense verbs in the following example.

e.g.   During the experiment, two groups of people **participated** by driving in a simulator. One group **consisted** of people who were driving while talking on a cell phone. The other group **included** a group of people who were driving with a passenger in the car.

2.   The past and present tenses should not be confused because the **present tense** expresses **facts or habitual actions**, not **past events** such as in the following **boldfaced** example.

e.g.   Physicians **acknowledge** that young people **heal** faster than the elderly.

Typically, the past tense is formed by placing "d" or "ed" at the end of the verb.

I yell**ed** for help.   We interview**ed** 6,000 patients.

You examine**d** the young participants.

The researcher conclude**d** that young   The patients receive**d** pain killers.
people are more likely to have accidents.

Irregular Verbs in the Past Tense

In English, many verbs have irregular forms in the past tense. To be a good writer, you must spell and use irregular verbs accurately. To assist you in meeting these goals, a complete list of the most common irregular verbs in English is provided in Appendix A.

Frequent Errors in the Use of Irregular Past Tense Verbs

This section reviews some common errors students make in using irregular past tense verbs.

1. Was and Were

    When you use the verb *to be* in the past tense, the subject must agree with the verb. For instance, if the subject is singular (I, he, she, or it), use the word *was*, but if it is plural (you, we or they), use *were*.

    > e.g.   Ana *was* late today.
    >
    > She *was* a difficult person.
    >
    > We *were* annoyed.
    >
    > You *were* never on time for class.

2. Bought and Brought

    The word *bought* is the past tense of the verb *buy*, and *brought* is the past tense of *bring*. Note how these words are used in the following examples.

    > (bring: past tense) Jose <u>*brought*</u> his books to his friend's house.
    >
    > (buy: past tense) I <u>*bought*</u> a new laptop computer last year.

3. Fell and Felt

    The past tense of the word *feel* is *felt*. *Fell* is the past tense of the verb *fall*. Observe the following examples.

    > (feel: past tense) The man <u>*felt*</u> a sharp pain in his chest.
    >
    > (fall: past tense) The child <u>*fell*</u> down on the cracked sidewalk.

4. Thought, Through, and Though

    The word *thought* is the past tense of the verb *think*, and it can be a noun, too. However, the word *through* is a preposition.

Finally, *though* is a danger word that creates a dependent adverbial clause. Note the use of these words in the following examples.

(think: past tense verb) We *thought* we passed the test.

(thought: noun) The president's *thoughts* were unclear.

(through: preposition) The woman ran *through* a thousand dollars in Las Vegas.

(though: subordinating conjunction) *Though* Mario disliked Luigi, he was polite.

5. Taught and Thought

The word *taught* is the past tense of the verb *teach*. However, the word *thought* is the past tense of the verb *think,* and as mentioned previously, the word *thought* can also function as a noun. Observe the following examples.

(teach: past tense) She *taught* English composition for years.

(think: past tense verb) He *thought* before he responded.

(thought: noun) Many *thoughts* were flying through my head.

6. Threw and Through

The word *threw* is the past tense of the verb *throw*. However, as mentioned previously, the word *through* is a preposition. Observe the following examples.

(throw: past tense verb) Santana *threw* the ball.

(through: preposition) She went *through* this ordeal for years.

7. Send and Sent

The word *send* is the present tense and the simple form of the verb. However, *sent* is the past tense and the past participle of the verb.

(send: present tense) We *send* Katerina fruit for her birthday.

(sent: past tense) Last month we *sent* her roses instead of fruit.

(sent: past participle) The professor had *sent* the students e-mails before.

8. Build and Built

The word *build* is the present tense and the simple form of the verb; however, *built* is the past tense and the past participle.

(build: present tense) Those companies *build* houses in New York.

97

(built: past tense) Mr. Trump *built* Trump Towers.

9. Catch and Caught

When using the past tense, you may be tempted to add the letters *ed* on the end of the word *catch*; however, this form is incorrect. The past tense of the word *catch* is *caught*.

(catch: present tense) They *catch* the ball during the baseball game.

(caught: past tense) The child *caught* a bad cold.

10. Meet and Met

Many writers confuse the present tense verb *meet* with the past tense verb *met*. One trick that assists writers in selecting the correct word is to remember that the past tense verb *met* rhymes with words such as *bet, get, jet, let, net, pet, set,* and *wet*, while the present tense verb form, *meet*, rhymes with *beet,* and *feet*.

(meet: present tense) My class *meets* at 10 o'clock every morning.

(met: past tense) My husband *met* his boss for lunch.

11. Went and When

Because the words *when* and *went* are close in pronunciation, many students confuse the two words when they write. The past tense of the verb *go* is *went*. On the other hand, the word *when* is used to ask a question of time, or it can also function as a relative pronoun in a noun clause.

(went: past tense of go) She *went* to the opera on her birthday.

(when: question word) *When* is the final exam?

(when: relative pronoun) We always liked it *when* my mother made a cake.

Error Analyses

Read each of the following paragraphs and correct any mistakes in the underlined words, which use the present, present progressive, or the past tenses.

1.   When drivers talked on cell phones, it causes traffic accidents. Drivers needed to be

more attentive when they driving a car. A car can be a dangerous weapon if it is not driven

with caution. According to the police department, more than 40 percent of the accidents

<u>involve</u> drivers on cell phones and this problem <u>is increase</u> because almost everyone <u>owned</u> a cell phone. As a result, the accident rate <u>increased</u> annually. When a driver <u>using</u> a cell phone, it <u>puts</u> the driver, the passengers, and pedestrians in danger. When my friend <u>when</u> away to college, his father <u>died</u> in an accident because a teenager was text messaging and driving the car at a high speed. This man's life can never be brought back, but reckless driving can be prevented, if we <u>ask</u> our lawmakers and police department to enforce the laws that ban talking or texting on cell phones while a person <u>is driving</u> a motor vehicle.

2.   When I <u>was</u> a child, my father <u>used</u> to spank me when I <u>disobeyed</u> him. But, I frequently <u>didn't understanded</u> what I had done wrong. Moreover, I <u>fell</u> terribly hurt when he <u>done</u> this to me. Psychologists <u>believe</u> that spanking <u>didn't prevent</u> negative behavior, but it can sometimes incite worse behavior. For instance, when I <u>when</u> to the supermarket, I <u>seen</u> a mother hit her little boy for taking a piece of candy and eating it. The child <u>yelled</u> when she <u>striked</u> him, but when she <u>turn</u> her back, he <u>hitted</u> his baby sister. I can only imagine what will happen when this little boy <u>get</u> older and <u>is</u> more powerful.

Vocabulary

Many developmental writers have good vocabularies, but they struggle to use them appropriately in their writing. Since the CATW test will examine the use of language and vocabulary, it is important to learn how to edit your writing so that you use clear, appropriate vocabulary. In each of the following sentences, inappropriate or unclear vocabulary is used. Read the sentences and try to revise them so that they are clearer and easier to understand. Also, note that after you change one word, it is sometimes necessary to revise others words. Observe how the wording is revised in the following example.

               return   *need*   *to fit*

e.g.   Even after soldiers ~~are back~~ from a war safely, they ~~have to spend~~ time ~~fitting~~ back into

                                                 skills

the society, and they have to learn new ~~things~~ in order to survive.

1. Even if a soldier can get a decent income by participating in a war, his emotional burden is more weighed than the money.

2. Every criminal is supposed to hire a lawyer to help go through their cases. However, not everyone has plenty of money to hire the best lawyer to prevent the punishment. Therefore, poor people who have no money get a free newbie attorney who may not be competent. Many of the free lawyers don't have much experience helping people win their case.

3. New York City has a huge mass transportation system. It can go from using buses, trains, and even airports. Therefore, residents in the City can travel everywhere because the transportation system is very nice.

4. After I got rejective from Queens College, I decided to come to a community college. No matter what career a person wants to enter, there is always a college to start in NYC.

5. I was hit by a reckless driver on a cell phone. The driver made a right turn without indicating because his other hand was on his phone. Some drivers allow their cell phones to consume them so that their reactions are hampered.

6. Drivers should not use their hand-held cell phones while driving on the route because it can be costly when the driver receives fines and points on his/her license. When my friend was caught talking on his phone while he was driving, he received a ticket and points on his license. This raised his car insurance at a high price. Since he couldn't spend that much money on the insurance, he sold his car.

7. My work is using a sharp knife to make the old parts from machines so that they can be replaced with new parts.

8. Good waiters have to be walking around their section of tables at lease every five minutes to see if their customers need attention. If the waiter develops a good job, he/she can get better tips. However, some waiters avoid their customers by gathering in a corner to chat with the other servers, and this affects the waiters' tips.

9. If in a family just the husband gets money, his money may not be enough to support his family.

10. When I came to this country, I gave up my citizenship from my homeland, and sword an oath to the United States of America. (Answers [6])

Answer Key for Chapter Four

If you selected choice <u>c</u>, you are correct.
first main clause + semi-colon + conjunctive adjective + comma + main clause
comma
Answer b
Answer c
Answers are as follows.

1. Even if a soldier ~~can get~~ *earns* a decent income by ~~participating~~ *fighting* in a war, his emotional burden ~~is more weighed than~~ *outweighs* the money.

2. Every criminal is supposed to hire a lawyer to ~~help go through their cases~~ *defend him/her*. However, not everyone has ~~plenty of~~ *enough* money to hire the best lawyer to ~~prevent the punishment~~ *get a good defense*. Therefore, poor people who have no money get a ~~free newbie~~ *legal aid* attorney who may not be competent. Many of the free lawyers don't have much experience helping people ~~win their case~~ *defend themselves*.

3. New York City has a huge mass transportation system. It ~~can go from using~~ *includes* buses, trains and even airports. Therefore, residents in the City can travel everywhere because the transportation system is ~~very nice~~ *so extensive*.

4. After I got ~~rejective~~ *rejected* from Queens College, I decided to ~~come to~~ *enroll in* a community college. No matter what the career a person wants to enter, there is always a college ~~to start~~ *that has this major* in NYC.

5. I was hit by a reckless driver *who was conversing* on a cell phone. The driver made a right turn without ~~indicating~~ *signaling* because his other hand was on his phone. Some drivers allow their cell phones to consume them so that their reactions are hampered.

6. Drivers should not use their hand-held cell phones while driving on the ~~route~~ *road* because it can be costly when the driver receives fines and points on his/her license. When my friend was caught talking on his phone while he was driving, he received a ticket and points on his license. This *ticket and points* ~~raised~~ *doubled* his car insurance ~~at a high price~~. Since he couldn't ~~spend that much money~~ *afford the increased rate* on the insurance, he sold his car.

7. My work ~~is using~~ *requires me to use* a sharp knife to ~~make~~ *remove* the old parts from machines so that they can be replaced with new parts.

102

8. Good waiters ~~have to be walking~~ *circulate* around their section of tables at ~~lease~~ *least* every five minutes to see if their customers need attention. If the waiter ~~develops a good job~~ *provides good service,* he/she can get better tips. However, some waiters ~~avoid~~ *ignore* their customers by gathering in a corner to chat with the other servers, and this *behavior* effects the waiters' tips.

9. *In a family,* if ~~in a family~~ just the husband ~~gets~~ *earns* money, his ~~money~~ *income* may not be enough to support his family.

Appendix A

Simple form of verb	Simple Present Tense	Simple Past Tense	Past Participle
be	am/is/are	was, were	been
become		became	become
begin		began	begun
bend		bent	bent
bite		bit	bitten
blow		blew	blown
break		broke	broken
bring		brought	brought
build		built	built
buy		bought	bought
catch		caught	caught
choose		chose	chosen
cling		clung	clung
come		came	come
cost		cost	cost
cut		cut	cut
dig		dug	dug
do	do/does	did	done
draw		drew	drawn
drink		drank	drunk
drive		drove	driven
eat		ate	eaten
fall		fell	fallen
feed		fed	fed
feel		felt	felt
fight		fought	fought
find		found	found
flee		fled	fled
fling		flung	flung

Simple Form of Verb	Simple Present Tense	Simple Past Tense	Past Participle
fly		flew	flown
forbid		forbade	forbidden
forget		forgot	forgotten
forgive		forgave	forgiven
freeze		froze	frozen
get		got	gotten
give		gave	given
go	go/goes	went	gone
grind		ground	ground
grow		grew	grown
hang		hung	hung
have	has/have	had	had
hear		heard	heard
hide		hid	hidden
hit		hit	hit
hold		held	held
hurt		hurt	hurt
keep		kept	kept
kneel		knelt	knelt
know		knew	known
lay		laid	laid
lead		led	led
leap		leapt	leapt
leave		left	left
lend		lent	lent
let		let	let
lie		lay	lain
light		lit	lit
lose		lost	lost
make		made	made

Simple Form of Verb	Simple Present Tense	Simple Past Tense	Past Participle
mean		meant	meant
meet		met	met
pay		paid	paid
prove		proved	proved/proven
put		put	put
quit		quit	quit
read		read	read
ride		rode	ridden
ring		rang	rung
rise		rose	risen
run		ran	run
say		said	said
see		saw	seen
seek		sought	sought
sell		sold	sold
send		sent	sent
set		set	set
sew		sewed	sewn/sewed
shake		shook	shaken
shoot		shot	shot
shut		shut	shut
smg		sang	sung
sit		sat	sat
sleep		slept	slept
slide		slid	slid
speak		spoke	spoken
speed		sped	sped
spend		spent	spent
spill		spilt	spilt
stand		stood	stood

Simple Form of Verb	Simple Present Tense	Simple Past Tense	Past Participle
Steal		Stole	stolen
stick		stuck	stuck
strike		struck	stricken
swear		swore	sworn
sweep		swept	swept
swim		swam	swum
take		took	taken
teach		taught	taught
tear		tore	torn
tell		told	told
think		thought	thought
throw		threw	thrown
understand		understood	understood
wake		woke	woken
wear		wore	worn
weave		wove	woven
win		won	won
wind		wound	wound
withdraw		withdrew	withdrawn
write		wrote	written

References

Bailey, Alyssa. (2010, May 23). Five fast ways to 'unspoil' your child. *USA Weekend Magazine*. Retrieved from http://www.usaweekend.com/article/20100521/HOME01/5230320/5-fast-ways-to-unspoil-your-child

Berlin, Adam. (2008, October 22). Social promotion or retention? Finding a middle ground should start in middle schools. *Education Week*. Retrieved from http://www.edweek.org/login.html?source=http://www.edweek.org/ew/articles/2008/10/22/09berlin.h28.html&destination=http://www.edweek.org/ew/articles/2008/10/22/09berlin.h28.html&levelId=2100

Bilton, Nick. (2012, June 18). An E-Book Fan, Missing the Smell of Paper and Glue. *The New York Times*. Retrieved from http://bits.blogs.nytimes.com/2012/06/18/caught-between-nostalgia-for-print-and-the-practicality-of-digital/

Bilton, Nick. (2012, July 8). Disruptions: Life's too short for so much e-mail. *The New York Times*. Retrieved from http://bits.blogs.nytimes.com/2012/07/08/life%E2%80%99s-too-short-for-so-much-e-mail/?pagewanted=print

Carey, Benedict. (2010, September 7). Forget what you know about good study habits. *The New York Times*. Retrieved from http://www.nytimes.com/2010/09/07/health/views/07mind.html?ref=mind&pagewanted=print

Daily Mail Reporter. (2010, Nov. 5). What You've Never Had, You Never Miss: Canadian Couple who Won $11.2m in the Lottery Gives It ALL away to Charity. Retrieved from http://www.dailymail.co.uk/news/article-1326473/Canadian-couple-Allen-Violet-Large-away-entire-11-2m-lottery-win.html

Hamilton, John. (2008, October 28). Think you're multitasking? Think again. *NPR.org*.

Retrieved from http://www.npr.org/templates/story/story.php?storyId=95256794

Harris, Gardiner. (2010, February 7). A federal effort to push junk food out of schools. *The New York Times*. Retrieved from

http://www.nytimes.com/2010/02/08/health/nutrition/08junk.html?pagewanted=print

Heffernan, Virginia. (2011, January 9). Against headphones. *The New York Times*. Retrieved

from http://www.nytimes.com/2011/01/09/magazine/09FOB-medium-

t.html?_r=1&pagewanted=print

Hirshey, Gerri. (2009, December 9). Teenagers and cars: A deadly mix. *The New York Times*.

Retrieved from

http://www.nytimes.com/2007/12/09/nyregion/nyregionspecial2/09RTEEN.html?scp=10

&sq=how%20to%20keep%20teens%20safe%20behind%20the%20wheel&st=cse

Hoxworth, Laura. (2010, August 29). Stop multi-tasking and do more. *USA Weekend*. Retrieved

from http://www.usaweekend.com/fdcp/?12831097680999

Kulla, Bridget. (2009, March 4). Advantages of community colleges. *Fastweb*. Retrieved from

http://www.fastweb.com/college-search/articles/22-advantages-of-attending-a-

community-college

Learned self-reliance: The negative effects of spoiling children. (2009, April 4). *Intent.com*.

retrieved from http://www.intent.com/blog/2009/04/09/learned-self-reliance-negative-

effects-spoiling-children

Mankiw, N. Gregory. (2010, September 5). A course load for the game of life. *New York Times*.

Retrieved from

http://www.nytimes.com/2010/09/05/business/economy/05view.html?_r=1&ref=business

5

Middle earth: Parenting with youth for a responsible adulthood. (2010, September 9). Bullying

and problem solving. *WorldPress.com.* Retrieved from

http://middleearthnj.wordpress.com/2010/09/12/bullying-and-problem-solving/

New York Newsday. (2011, June 16). Study: Facebook users are users friendlier. Retrieved from

http://www.newsday.com/study-facebook-users-friendlier-trusting-1.2963217

Neistat, Casey. (2012, January 9). Texting while walking. *The New York Times.* Retrieved from

http://www.nytimes.com/2012/01/09/opinion/texting-while-

walking.html?_r=1&ref=technology

Parker-Pope, Tara. (2008, December 12). Chatty driving: Phones vs. passengers. *The New York*

Times. Retrieved from http://well.blogs.nytimes.com/2008/12/01/chatty-driving-phones-

vs-passengers/?scp=31&sq=texting%20and%20%22Tara%20Parker-Pope%22&st=cse

Parker-Pope, Tara. (2008, August 18). Getting through to teens about driving risks. *The New*

York Times. Retrieved from http://well.blogs.nytimes.com/2008/08/18/getting-through-

to-teens-about-driving-

risks/?scp=1&sq=Getting%20Through%20to%20Teens%20About%20Driving%20Risks

&st=cse

Parker-Pope, Tara. (2007, October 3). How to keep teens safe behind the wheel. *The New York*

Times. Retrieved from http://well.blogs.nytimes.com/2007/10/03/how-to-keep-teens-safe-

behind-the-

wheel/?scp=3&sq=Driving%20Safety%20Programs%20for%20Teens&st=cse

Parker-Pope, Tara. (2010, January 26). Marriage and women over forty. *The New York Times.* Retrieved from http://well.blogs.nytimes.com/2010/01/26/marriage-and-women-over-40/?scp=2&sq=hedonic%20marriage&st=cse

Parker-Pope, Tara. (2010, May 3). New bold warnings on tobacco ads. *The New York Times.* Retrieved from http://well.blogs.nytimes.com/2010/05/03/new-bold-warnings-on-tobacco-ads/

Parker-Pope, Tara. (2010, January 22). She works. They're happy. *The New York Times.* Retrieved from http://www.nytimes.com/2010/01/24/fashion/24marriage.html?scp=3&sq=married%20women%20work%20happier&st=cse

Parker-Pope, Tara. (2010, April 6). Surprisingly, family time has grown. *The New York Times.* Retrieved from http://query.nytimes.com/gst/fullpage.html?res=9E05E0DC113AF935A35757C0A9669D8B63&scp=4&sq=hedonic%20marriage&st=cse

Parker-Pope, Tara. (2010, February 9). Commercials are the culprit in TV obesity link. *The New York Times.* Retrieved from http://well.blogs.nytimes.com/2010/02/09/commercials-are-the-culprit-in-tv-obesity-link/?scp=1&sq=Commercials%20Are%20the%20Culprit%20in%20TV-Obesity%20Link&st=cse

Parker-Pope, Tara. (2010, January 23). The changing economics of marriage. *The New York Times.* Retrieved from http://well.blogs.nytimes.com/2010/01/23/the-changing-economics-of-marriage/?scp=8&sq=married%20women%20work%20happier&st=cse

Paul, Pamela. (2010, July 11). Does moving a child create adult baggage? *The New York Times*.

    Retrieved from

    http://www.nytimes.com/2010/07/11/fashion/11StudiedMoving.html?_r=1&sq=moving

    often and children&st=cse&scp=3&pagewanted=print

Rampell, Catherine. (2010, October 19). Going on a diet? Start paying in cash. *The New York*

    Times. Retrieved from http://economix.blogs.nytimes.com/2010/10/19/going-on-a-diet-

    start-paying-in-cash/?pagemode=print

Richtel, Matt. (2010, November 21). Achieving a healthful digital diet. *The New York Times*.

    Retrieved from

    http://www.nytimes.com/2010/11/21/technology/21brainside.html?_r=1&pagewanted=pr

    int

Rockler-Gladen, Naomi. (2007, January 17). Community colleges advantages and disadvantages

    of the two-year junior college experience. *Suite 101.com Insightful writers Informed*

    Readers. Retrieved from http://www.suite101.com/content/community-colleges-a11880

Shippee, Steven. (2004, October 8). N.Y.C. Retention plan draws mixed response. *Education*

    Week. Retrieved from http://www.edweek.org/ew/articles/2004/10/06/06letter-

    5.h24.html?tkn=LSTFMue2Guqv9fxxLGIiydwHzMfNWTw5djJ%2B&print=1

Steinberg, Jacques. (2010, May 14). Plan B: Skip college. *The New York Times*. Retrieved from

    http://www.nytimes.com/2010/05/16/weekinreview/16steinberg.html?pagewanted=print

The US Department of Justice. (n.d.). What are identity theft and identity fraud? Retrieved from

    http://www.justice.gov/criminal/fraud/websites/idtheft.html#whatcommonways

Tierney, John. (2006, February 28). The happiest wives. *The New York Times.* Retrieved from

    http://select.nytimes.com/2006/02/28/opinion/28tierney.html?_r=1&scp=2&sq=married

    %20women%20work%20happier&st=cse

Wagner, Kurt. (2011, Sept. 17). Distracted: Are you paying $75 an hour to sit in class and check

    Facebook? *USA Today: College.* Retrieved from

    http://www.usatodayeducate.com/staging/index.php/ccp/distracted-are-you-paying-75-

    an-hour-sit-in-class-and-check-facebook#.TngEpoXtL3k.facebook

Warner, Judith. (2010, May 28). The why-worry generation. *The New York Times.* Retrieved

    from http://www.nytimes.com/2010/05/30/magazine/30fob-wwln-

    t.html?_r=2&sq=generation&pagewanted=print

Weiner, Eric. (2009, July 19). Lowered expectations. *The New York Times.* Retrieved from

    http://opinionator.blogs.nytimes.com/2009/07/19/lowered-

    expectations/?scp=7&sq=hedonic%20marriage&st=cse

Westchester Institute for Human Services Research. (1998). The balanced view: Social

    promotion and retention. Retrieved from

    http://www.sharingsuccess.org/code/socprom.html

CPSIA information can be obtained at www.ICGtesting.com
Printed in the USA
LVOW02s2003080615

441069LV00004B/4/P